American Presidents

in World History

Titles in the series

American Presidents
in World History

VOLUME 5

LYNDON B. JOHNSON TO GEORGE W. BUSH

GREENWOOD PRESS
Westport, Connecticut · London

Library of Congress Cataloging-in-Publication Data

Creative Media Applications
American presidents in world history.
    p. cm. — (Middle school reference)
   Includes bibliographical references and index.
   ISBN 0–313–32564–2 (set : alk. paper)—0–313–32565–0
(v.1)—0–313–32566–9 (v.2)—0–313–32567–7 (v.3)—0–313–32568–5
(v.4)—0–313–32569–3 (v.5)
    1. Presidents—United States—Biography—Juvenile literature.
2. Presidents—United States—History—Juvenile literature. 3. United States—Politics and
government—Decision making—Juvenile literature. 4. United States—Foreign relations—
Decision making—Juvenile literature. 5. World politics—Juvenile literature. I. Series.
E176.1.A6568 2003
973'.09'9—dc21   2002035205
[B]

British Library Cataloguing in Publication Data is available.

Library of Congress Catalog Card Number: 2002035205
ISBN: 0–313–32564–2 (set)
        0–313–32565–0 (Vol. 1)
        0–313–32566–9 (Vol. 2)
        0–313–32567–7 (Vol. 3)
        0–313–32568–5 (Vol. 4)
        0–313–32569–3 (Vol. 5)

First published in 2003

Greenwood Press, 88 Post Road West, Westport, CT 06881
An imprint of Greenwood Publishing Group, Inc.
www.greenwood.com

Printed in the United States of America

♾™

The paper used in this book complies with the
Permanent Paper Standard issued by the National
Information Standards Organization (Z39.48–1984).

10 9 8 7 6 5 4 3 2 1

A Creative Media Applications, Inc. Production
Writer: Michael Burgan
Design and Production: Alan Barnett, Inc.
Editor: Matt Levine
Copyeditor: Laurie Lieb
Proofreader: Shana Grob
Indexer: Nara Wood
Associated Press Photo Researcher: Yvette Reyes
Consultant: Dr. Melvin I. Urofsky, Virginia Commonwealth University

Photo credits:
Cover, iii: © CORBIS
AP/Wide World Photographs *pages:* viii, 3, 4, 6, 8, 10, 11, 12, 17, 19, 20, 21, 22, 25, 26, 30, 32, 34, 36,
   37, 40, 42, 44, 48, 50, 52, 53, 56, 58, 61, 65, 67, 69, 70, 71, 72, 77, 78, 80, 82, 84, 86, 88, 89, 92, 94,
   96, 98, 100, 101, 102, 104, 106, 109, 110, 112, 114, 116, 119, 121, 123
© NATO Photos *page:* 46
Alan Barnett *page:* 118
Library of Congress photo archives: Johnson — LC-USZ62-13036 DLC, *page* 1;
   Nixon — LC-USZ62-13037 DLC, *page* 15; Ford — LC-USZ62-13038 DLC, *page* 29;
   Carter — LC-USZ62-13039 DLC, *page* 39; Reagan — LC-USZ62-13040 DLC, *page* 57;
   Bush (Sr.) — LC-USZ62-98302 DLC, *page* 75; Clinton — LC-USZ62-107700 DLC, *page* 91

Table of Contents

Introduction

Under the U.S. Constitution, both the president and Congress play a role in managing the foreign relations of the United States. Foreign relations are dealings with foreign countries, including such issues as trade and military matters.

The president serves as the commander in chief of the military when it is "called into the actual service of the United States." The president can also negotiate treaties with foreign powers, although the Senate has final approval on their wording. The president selects the people who will represent the country overseas, as well—again with Senate approval. For advice on foreign affairs, the president often turns to the secretary of state, the government's chief diplomat. The State Department is not mentioned in the Constitution, but it was created by Congress in 1789.

Helping the president conduct foreign relations are a number of agencies. These include the Central Intelligence Agency (CIA), the country's chief foreign spy service, and the National Security Council (NSC). The NSC includes the secretary of state and the national security adviser. The council works for the president alone.

Under the Constitution, Congress has the power to "regulate commerce with foreign nations," including collecting taxes on goods brought into the United States. The lawmakers are also charged with providing for the country's defense, and only Congress can declare war against a foreign enemy.

When America's political leaders shaped the Constitution, they seem to have expected Congress to play a major role in foreign relations, with the president carrying out the lawmakers' instructions. Over time, however, presidents have greatly expanded their power in many areas, including foreign relations. In 1803, for example, Thomas Jefferson wanted to buy Louisiana from France, but he hesitated, since the Constitution did not specifically give the president the right to buy foreign lands. In the end, he acted on his own, deciding that the purchase was too important to pass up. Other presidents have also chosen to see implied, or unstated, powers in the Constitution that justified their acting on their own when they felt it was necessary.

Presidential activity in foreign relations became especially notable in military affairs. Instead of waiting for Congress to call the military into service, presidents began sending troops overseas on their own, asserting their power as commander in chief. This pattern became most common in the twentieth century. In the Korean War (1950–1953), for example, President Harry Truman sent more than 1 million troops into battle without asking Congress to declare war. Truman called the conflict a "police action."

Some of the rise in presidential power came as U.S. foreign policy changed. In 1796, George Washington cautioned the country to have "as little political connection as possible" with foreign nations and concentrate on its own affairs. However, powerful European nations played a large role in the Western Hemisphere (North and South America). Their activity sometimes threatened U.S. interests. The desire of the United States to trade around the world also brought it into conflict with other nations.

The Oval Office in the White House is the president's official workplace. Here many decisions are made that affect global politics. The presidential seal in the center symbolizes the president's power and position.

By the 1860s, some U.S. presidents and diplomats were eager to acquire new lands for the country. The United States soon became an imperial nation with its own colonies, just like Great Britain, France, and others. By the early twentieth century, the United States was a major economic power, and its leaders began shaping an internationalist foreign policy. Woodrow Wilson, more than any other president before him, set the country on this path. Americans would try to bring democracy to other countries and would fight, when necessary, to defend U.S. interests. Still, some Americans remained isolationists, arguing that the United States should stay out of foreign affairs as much as possible.

The two world wars of the twentieth century confirmed the position of the United States as the chief defender of democracy and free enterprise. In that role, it led the battle against Communism during the Cold War. In 1991, the world's most powerful Communist nation, the Soviet Union, collapsed. The United States was left as the only true superpower—a nation able to exercise its military might anywhere in the world. Being a superpower has risks, as Americans learned in the 1990s. Efforts to build democracy abroad sometimes failed. Some people saw the United States as a global bully, ignoring the interests of other nations.

Terrorists from the Middle East and Africa began attacking U.S. buildings and military forces, hoping to weaken the influence of the United States in their homelands. They also sought to spread their own form of Islam, a religion born in the Middle East. While facing the danger of terrorism, U.S. presidents also faced off against more traditional enemies—foreign countries that threatened U.S. interests.

The five volumes of *American Presidents in World History* tell the story of America's presidents and their role in America's rise to world power. Each president has faced international problems; some have done better than others in solving them. Here are the failures and successes of American diplomacy during often-difficult times.

Note: All metric conversions in this book are approximate.

Lyndon B. Johnson

THIRTY-SIXTH PRESIDENT

FACT FILE

NAME
Lyndon Baines Johnson

DATE OF BIRTH
August 27, 1908

PLACE OF BIRTH
Stonewall, Texas

POLITICAL PARTY
Democratic

VICE PRESIDENT
Hubert H. Humphrey

YEARS AS PRESIDENT
1963–1969

SECRETARY OF STATE
Dean Rusk

DATE OF DEATH
January 22, 1973

★ ★ ★

A Difficult Presidency

As a boy, Lyndon B. Johnson thought about becoming president of the United States. He entered politics at an early age and eventually became one of the most powerful leaders ever in the U.S. Senate. When he finally reached the White House, however, Johnson could not celebrate as he might have if he had won an election. As vice president, Johnson took over the presidency in the dark days after the assassination of John F. Kennedy.

As president, Johnson moved forward with some of Kennedy's policies. He strengthened civil rights and provided new government services to the elderly and the poor. In Vietnam, however, Johnson continued a policy that was drawing the United States deeper into a war that would be difficult to win. Despite Johnson's successes at home, the Vietnam War (1964–1975) ended Johnson's career in politics.

From Texas to Washington

As a child in Texas, Lyndon Johnson sometimes rode with his father, Sam Ealy Johnson Jr., as he visited voters in the region. The elder Johnson twice served in the Texas state legislature. Lyndon's family was not wealthy. However, Lyndon's mother, Rebekah, always stressed the value of education, and Lyndon did well in school.

For several years after high school, Johnson traveled and worked. In 1927, Johnson entered Southwest Texas State Teachers College in San Marcos. He graduated in 1930 with a degree in history and took a job teaching in Houston. He also began working for a local politician, Welly K. Hopkins, who was running for the state senate in Texas. After helping Hopkins win his election, Johnson received a call from Richard Kleberg, a Democrat who had just been elected to the U.S. House of Representatives. He asked Johnson to serve as his secretary, and in 1932, Johnson left for Washington, D.C.

In his new job, Johnson worked long hours helping Kleberg. Not all his time, however, was spent at work. In 1934, on a trip back to Texas, Johnson met Claudia "Lady Bird" Taylor. Within two months, she and Johnson were married, and Lady Bird joined Johnson in Washington.

The next year, Johnson returned home to take a new job, as director of the National Youth Administration (NYA) in Texas. This government agency's goal was to help young people find jobs or continue their schooling. By this time, the country was suffering through the Great Depression, when millions of Americans lost their jobs and their homes. As director of the NYA, Johnson made sure that young Texans received their fair share of the government's aid.

On to Congress

In 1937, Johnson won his first political race, gaining a seat in the U.S. House of Representatives. In 1941, he hoped to move up to the U.S. Senate, but he lost a close race.

That December, the United States entered World War II (1939–1945) after the Japanese bombed U.S. naval ships at Pearl Harbor, Hawaii. Johnson was the first member of Congress to join the military. He briefly served in the Pacific, reporting back to Washington on the fighting in the region, before returning to Congress.

Johnson served in the House of Representatives through World War II and into the start of the Cold War. The Cold War was a competition between the Soviet Union and the United States to spread their influence and political belief around the globe. Johnson wanted to keep a strong military, and he supported President Harry Truman's policy of containing the spread of *Communism,* the political and economic system promoted by the Soviet Union. The United States and the Soviet Union were

FAST FACT

President Franklin D. Roosevelt's program to help people during the Great Depression was called the New Deal. The NYA was just one of many New Deal agencies that tried to put people to work.

Lieutenant Commander Lyndon Johnson (right) served in the Pacific as a naval officer. Here Johnson is greeted by Brigadier General Martin F. Scanlon and General Ralph Royce in New Guinea. Johnson survived two airplane crashes while in New Guinea and was awarded the Silver Star for gallantry.

Lyndon Johnson meets with other members of the Senate Armed Forces Committee in 1951 to discuss military personnel needs. Johnson was a strong supporter of the military during his Senate career.

considered *superpowers*—they had military strength that no other countries could match.

In 1947, Greece was going through a civil war in which Communist forces played an important role. At the same time, Turkey faced a military threat from the Soviet Union. In Congress, Johnson spoke in favor of Truman's plan to send aid to Greece and Turkey.

In 1948, Johnson was elected to the U.S. Senate. In the Senate, he served on the Armed Forces Committee and continued to call for a strong military. When the Korean War (1950–1953) started in June 1950, Johnson pledged to help the U.S. war effort.

In 1952, Dwight Eisenhower's presidential victory helped the Republicans take control of the Senate. The Democrats, now the minority party, chose Johnson as their leader. When the Democrats regained control of the Senate in 1954, Johnson became the majority leader—the most important position in that body. He played a large role in deciding which bills would be debated and on which senate committees senators would serve.

On the whole, Johnson supported President Eisenhower's handling of the Cold War. By the late 1950s, however, Johnson and other Democrats thought that the Republicans had let the Soviet Union take the lead in several important areas. The Democrats claimed that the Soviets had built more long-range missiles than the United States. These intercontinental ballistic missiles (ICBMs) could be used to carry nuclear warheads. The successful launch of the Soviet satellite *Sputnik* also concerned Johnson and his party. *Sputnik* was the first human-made object to orbit Earth. The majority leader led an investigation that claimed the Soviet Union was racing ahead of the United States in science and technology. In later years, the claims of the investigation were proven false.

From Vice President to President

In the summer of 1956, some leaders of the Democratic Party considered Johnson as a candidate for U.S. president. In the end, however, the party chose Adlai Stevenson. During the next four years, Johnson tried to position himself as a candidate for the 1960 election. When that campaign began, Johnson faced competition from another Democratic senator, John F. Kennedy. That summer, Kennedy won the Democratic nomination. He then asked Johnson to run with him as the candidate for vice president. In November, Kennedy beat Richard Nixon in a close presidential race, and Johnson became the thirty-seventh vice president of the United States.

When Kennedy and Johnson came to power, one particular concern was Southeast Asia, which includes Vietnam, Laos, and Cambodia. Vietnam had become an issue for the United States under President Truman. France had controlled Vietnam since the nineteenth century. At the end of World War II, the Vietnamese, led by Ho Chi Minh, had declared their independence, but

France was not ready to give up this colony. Truman had sent aid to help the French. Eisenhower continued this policy of aiding the French, and by 1954, the United States was paying for 78 percent of France's military efforts in Vietnam. Despite this help, the French lost their war against the Vietnamese.

When the war ended, Vietnam was split in two. The north, led by Ho, was friendly with the Soviet Union and China, while the United States backed the government in the south. Ho wanted a Communist government ruling all of Vietnam, and he was ready to fight to get his way. Eisenhower and Kennedy, who both opposed the spread of Communism in Southeast Asia, aided South Vietnam.

In May 1961, Kennedy sent Johnson on a trip to the region. The vice president met with the South Vietnamese president, Ngo Dinh Diem. Many South Vietnamese did not like Diem because he ruled as a dictator. U.S. leaders knew that Diem was not a good leader, but they supported him because he was strongly anti-Communist. Both

Vice President Johnson was greeted with full military honors when he visited Saigon in May 1961. Upon his return to Washington, Johnson recommended that the United States become more actively involved in the conflict between North and South Vietnam.

Kennedy and Johnson believed that the "domino theory" could come into play if South Vietnam lost to the Communists. According to this theory, if one country turned Communist, so would the other countries nearby.

When he returned to the United States, Johnson told Kennedy that the United States either had to take active steps against Communism in Southeast Asia or else "throw in the towel." Johnson added, "I recommend we proceed with a clear-cut and strong program of action."

Johnson's career as vice president came to a shocking end on November 22, 1963. That day, as President Kennedy rode through the streets of Dallas, Texas, an assassin named Lee Harvey Oswald shot and killed Kennedy. Within hours, a stunned Johnson had been sworn in as the thirty-sixth president of the United States. He promised to continue Kennedy's programs and honor all U.S. commitments "from South Vietnam to West Berlin."

Plunging Deeper into Vietnam

About a month before his assassination, Kennedy had approved a secret plan to remove Diem as the president of South Vietnam. Kennedy and his advisers hoped that a new ruler could win more popular support. They also wanted a leader in Vietnam more willing to follow U.S. orders, as Diem had often worked against American interests. The generals who replaced Diem, however, were not eager to wage all-out war against the Communists threatening their country. Finally, a leader emerged who seemed more willing to fight: General Nguyen Khanh. However, he did not remain in power long, and the United States was soon playing a more active role in the war.

Johnson's advisers came up with several ideas for fighting North Vietnam, which was aiding South Vietnamese rebels who supported Communism. These rebels were known as the Vietcong. One U.S. plan was to

Berlin Trip

While the United States was concerned with Communism in Asia, it also faced a crisis in Berlin, Germany. After World War II, Germany had been split into four zones, controlled by Great Britain, France, the United States, and the Soviet Union. Berlin, the capital, had been split the same way. During the late 1940s, the French, British, and American zones of Germany were combined into a new nation, West Germany. The Soviet zone became East Germany. Berlin was deep within East Germany. The city's western half was controlled by the United States and its allies, and the eastern half was controlled by the Communists.

During the summer of 1961, the Communists built a wall to keep East Germans from entering democratic West Berlin. The United States did not want to risk a war over the wall. To show continued U.S. support for West Berlin, President Kennedy sent Johnson to the city. As vice president, Johnson made many trips abroad, representing Kennedy and the nation.

President Johnson returned to South Vietnam in 1967. In this photograph, he is speaking to the U.S. troops at Cam Ranh Bay. General William Westmoreland, the commander of U.S. forces in South Vietnam, is at the right.

bomb North Vietnam and the trail used to supply the Vietcong with weapons. This route through the jungle and mountains was named for Ho Chi Minh. Johnson's advisers also considered using tactical nuclear weapons—small nuclear devices designed for the battlefield. Still, even as the United States made battle plans, Johnson also held secret talks with the North Vietnamese, trying to end the war. The talks failed when the United States insisted that the Vietcong could not play a role in any future South Vietnamese government.

In August 1964, U.S. naval ships took part in a spy mission in the Gulf of Tonkin, off North Vietnam. The ships came under enemy fire. Two nights later, the ships' crews once again thought that they were under attack from North Vietnamese ships. U.S. planes, however, could not see any enemy fire. Johnson used that supposed second attack as an excuse to bomb North Vietnam. He then asked Congress to approve further military actions. Congress responded with the Gulf of Tonkin Resolution, which gave Johnson the approval that he wanted.

At the time, Ho Chi Minh turned to both the Soviet Union and China for more military support. In South Vietnam, the Vietcong attacked several U.S. air bases. At first, Johnson responded by ordering more bombing raids on North Vietnam, but the bombs did not weaken the Communists' will to fight. Johnson faced a difficult decision. As he told his wife, "I can't get out. I can't finish with what I've got. So what…do I do?" The answer came on March 8, 1965, when the first U.S. ground troops—some 3,500 marines—landed in South Vietnam.

FAST FACT

Lyndon Johnson was the fourth vice president to take over for a president killed in office. In 1865, Andrew Johnson replaced Abraham Lincoln; in 1881, Chester A. Arthur stepped in for James A. Garfield; and Theodore Roosevelt became president in 1901, after the assassination of William McKinley.

War Abroad, Trouble at Home

In the 1964 presidential election, Johnson faced Barry Goldwater, a Republican senator from Arizona. Goldwater had talked openly about using nuclear weapons against the Soviet Union. During the race, Johnson suggested that Goldwater was too dangerous, too likely to start a war, to serve as president. Many Americans seemed to agree, as Johnson easily won the election, taking 61 percent of the votes.

Johnson's military commander in South Vietnam was General William Westmoreland. He soon asked Johnson for more troops. By the end of 1965, more than 180,000 Americans were in South Vietnam. Johnson's secretary of defense, Robert McNamara, visited South Vietnam around that time. He thought that the United States would have to send twice as many troops, and even then, there was no guarantee of winning the war.

The U.S. strategy relied on search-and-destroy missions. Troops left their bases to hunt for and attack Vietcong camps. They returned to their bases at night. The Vietcong often fled the camps before U.S. attacks, then returned when the soldiers left. The Vietcong had several advantages in the war. They controlled most of the countryside and could move freely. They also received help from South Vietnamese who opposed their government.

Ho Chi Minh (1890–1969)

In photographs, Ho Chi Minh looked like a friendly, white-haired grandfather, but as ruler of North Vietnam, he was quick to assert his power, and he never backed down from challenging the United States. Ho was both a Communist and a nationalist. He took help from the Soviet Union and China, but he wanted Vietnam to be independent of these two larger countries. He was also determined to reunite North and South Vietnam under his rule. At one time, at the end of World War II, Ho briefly worked for the U.S. government as a spy against the Japanese. When Ho later declared Vietnam's independence from France, he turned to President Truman for support. Truman, however, seeing Ho's ties to the Communists, opposed Ho's new government.

The Vietcong fought a *guerrilla* war—they dressed like civilians and lived with them. U.S. troops could not tell who was an enemy fighter and who was an innocent civilian. U.S. raids that destroyed homes and villages led more South Vietnamese to support the Vietcong.

As the war dragged on, President Johnson's military advisers wanted even more troops and the freedom to attack the Vietcong when they fled into neighboring countries. Some advisers also wanted more direct military action against North Vietnam. Johnson, however, did not want to risk drawing the Soviet Union or China deeper into the conflict. He was committed to fighting a "limited" war, but because the U.S. role was limited, no victory was in sight.

At first, polls showed that Americans supported Johnson's decisions on the war. Over time, however, as more U.S. soldiers fought and died and as Americans saw the horrors of the war reported on TV news every night, public opinion began to change. Young people began to protest the U.S. involvement in Southeast Asia. Some young men refused to enter the military when they were drafted. At antiwar marches, many protesters shouted, "Hey, hey, LBJ, how many kids did you kill today?" Johnson took offense at any criticism of his efforts in Vietnam.

Johnson also saw that the war was hurting his ability to pass laws that he wanted at home. Starting in 1964, he had called for a series of public-aid programs called the Great Society. He wanted to continue the kind of government help first started under Roosevelt's New Deal. At first, Johnson was successful with his programs. He introduced Medicare, which helped the elderly and disabled pay their medical bills, and Medicaid, which helped the poor. Food stamps helped poor families buy food, and schools received billions of dollars. Johnson's Great Society also included new civil rights laws. By 1967, however, Johnson was losing support both for his war effort and some of his Great Society plans. He also had less money to spend at home because the country was spending so much on the military.

Protests against the war grew. So did riots sparked by racial tensions. Since the 1950s, the civil rights movement,

led by the Reverend Martin Luther King Jr., had been trying to gain economic and political equality for African Americans. The movement's slow progress left blacks frustrated, as did police violence that targeted blacks and civil rights workers. In Selma, Alabama, in 1965, police attacked marchers several times. During that summer, riots erupted in Watts, a black neighborhood in Los Angeles, California. The next two summers frustrated African Americans rioted in several cities, with the worst violence in Detroit, Michigan. Johnson had to send in troops to restore order.

Other Trouble Spots

During Johnson's presidency, Vietnam was not his only international concern. Like Presidents Eisenhower and Kennedy, Johnson feared the influence of Cuban leader Fidel Castro in Latin America. Castro was a Communist.

In January 1964, rioters in Panama attacked U.S. citizens living in the Canal Zone. This zone included the Panama Canal, which the United States controlled. The canal links

FAST FACT

Today, Medicare provides medical insurance for almost 40 million Americans. People over sixty-five and some younger people with disabilities can enroll in the program. Medicaid helps 36 million people of all ages receive medical care.

Ousted Dominican president Juan Bosch listens to a radio broadcast about the coup that will return him to power in 1965. President Johnson sent U.S. troops to the Dominican Republic to help establish peace. Bosch was defeated by Joaquín Balaguer in the 1966 elections.

FAST FACT

The Dominican Republic is located on the eastern part of Hispaniola, an island about 75 miles (120 kilometers) west of Puerto Rico. The Dominican Republic shares the island with Haiti.

the Atlantic and Pacific Oceans. Without it, ships would have to sail thousands of miles around South America to get from one coast of the United States to the other. Johnson believed that Communists supported by Castro stirred up the Panamanian crowds. President Roberto Chiari of Panama let the rioting go on because he thought that the violence would convince Johnson to start new negotiations regarding the canal. U.S. troops were called in to fight Panamanian gunmen, and several people on both sides were killed. Johnson insisted that Chiari restore order before he would discuss future arrangements about the canal. Chiari agreed, and the two countries began talks that lasted for years, eventually agreeing that the United States would turn over control of the canal to Panama.

In 1965, Johnson faced a problem in the Dominican Republic. This Caribbean country had been ruled by a military leader who was assassinated in 1962. Dominicans then elected Juan Bosch in their first democratic vote in decades. Bosch was not a Communist, but he often opposed U.S. interests. The Dominican military then overthrew Bosch, and his supporters rebelled. Johnson sent 24,000 marines to the Dominican Republic to end the rebellion and support a pro-American government.

The Cold War was also underway in the Middle East. The United States supported Israel, while the Soviet Union backed several Arab countries. Early in June 1967, a war between Israel and the Arab states heightened tensions between the superpowers. In less than a week, Israel had won major battles and took control of new territory. A cease-fire was arranged, but on June 10, the Soviet Union accused the Israelis of breaking the peace and threatened to step in. Johnson responded by sending U.S. warships close to the scene. At the same time, Israel and the Arabs were drafting a new cease-fire agreement. This Six-Day War in the Middle East ended without the superpowers' direct involvement.

Shortly after the Six-Day War, Johnson had his first face-to-face meeting with a Soviet leader, Aleksei Kosygin. The two met in Glassboro, New Jersey, and discussed ways to reduce tensions in the Middle East. They also talked about limiting the development of new nuclear weapons. Both countries now had a number of hydrogen bombs and missile warheads. *Hydrogen bombs* are nuclear weapons that use a process called *fusion*, or the joining together of atoms, to create destructive energy. The two sides did not make any major agreements on nuclear weapons at Glassboro, but they promised to hold future talks.

No Road to Peace

Johnson tried several times to start peace talks with the North Vietnamese but failed each time. By the end of 1967, almost 500,000 U.S. troops were in South Vietnam. U.S. bombs and search-and-destroy raids had not weakened the enemy's desire to fight. More Americans felt that it was time to bring the troops home.

Bombs Away

The first major U.S. bombing operation in North Vietnam was called Rolling Thunder. Later bombing missions were called Linebacker and Menu. During the Vietnam War, the United States dropped more bombs than were used by both sides combined during World War II. U.S. planes also dropped chemicals called defoliants, which killed trees and other plants, making it easier to spot the enemy and their camps.

FAST FACT

Robert Kennedy, brother of President John F. Kennedy, was assassinated in June 1968 after making a political appearance in California while running for the 1968 presidential election.

The *Pueblo* Incident

During his last year as president, Johnson briefly confronted North Korea. In January 1968, the North Koreans captured the *Pueblo*, a U.S. spy ship operating off their coast. Three Americans died during the capture, and the rest of the crew were taken prisoner. The first diplomatic efforts to win the release of the crew failed, so Johnson sent 14,000 troops to South Korea (where thousands more were already stationed). The North Koreans threatened to put the Americans on trial as criminals, but Johnson was able to win their release by the end of the year.

Early the next year, the United States had suffered another difficult assault in Vietnam. January 31, 1968, was the Vietnamese New Year, called Tet. Starting the day before, the Vietcong and North Vietnamese forces launched surprise attacks on dozens of South Vietnamese cities. In the fighting that followed the Tet Offensive, the Communists lost some of their best fighters, but as Johnson admitted, the North Vietnamese and Vietcong won a victory off the battlefield. The huge surprise attack further weakened public support for the war in the United States.

By March 31, Johnson had made two important decisions. To restart the peace talks, he would stop most of the bombing in North Vietnam. He also announced that he would not run for a second full term as president. Instead of running a presidential race, Johnson wanted to focus on the war in Vietnam, but he also knew that his record on handling the war would make it difficult for him to win again.

During Johnson's last months as president, the United States and North Vietnam held their first official peace talks. (The earlier talks had been held in secret.) These talks, however, made little progress, even after Johnson stopped all bombing in North Vietnam (though not in neighboring Laos).

During his last year, Johnson also worked to improve relations with the Soviet Union. In July 1968, the United States joined the Soviet Union and dozens of other countries in signing a treaty intended to stop the spread of nuclear weapons.

Despite that small success, Johnson was most closely tied to the failed war in Vietnam. The fighting dragged on for several years after Johnson left office. He later wrote, "As I left the Presidency, I was aware that not everything I had done about Vietnam…had been correct." The war had divided Americans into opposing camps. Some people wanted to stop the spread of Communism at all costs. Others said that it was wrong to support the unpopular South Vietnam government and attack countries so far from the United States. The lessons learned from Vietnam are still debated today.

Richard Nixon

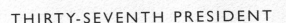

THIRTY-SEVENTH PRESIDENT

FACT FILE

NAME
Richard Milhous Nixon

DATE OF BIRTH
January 9, 1913

PLACE OF BIRTH
Yorba Linda, California

POLITICAL PARTY
Republican

VICE PRESIDENTS
Spiro Agnew (1969–1973)
Gerald Ford (1973–1974)

SECRETARIES OF STATE
William Rogers (1969–1973)
Henry Kissinger (1973–1974)

YEARS AS PRESIDENT
1969–1974

DATE OF DEATH
April 22, 1994

Presidential Highs and Lows

The presidency of Richard Nixon marked some of the major milestones of the Cold War. It also ended with Nixon resigning in disgrace, as he faced impeachment in the U.S. Congress. *Impeachment* is the legal process used to remove elected officials accused of committing a crime. Nixon was charged with covering up crimes by his staff and abusing his presidential powers.

Nixon had many critics during his political career. His supporters, however, point out that he opened up U.S. relations with Communist China, and he made the first meaningful attempts to limit the number of U.S. and Soviet nuclear weapons. He also ended the Vietnam War (1964–1975), though not before expanding it into neighboring Cambodia. Nixon was both flawed and skilled, one of the most complex men ever to sit as president of the United States.

Scholar and Lawyer

Nixon worked hard to achieve his success in politics. His family also worked hard, trying to prosper in California. His father, Frank, owned a lemon grove in Yorba Linda, but the farm failed. Frank Nixon then turned to carpentry, and later he and his wife, Hannah, opened a gas station and country store in Whittier. The Nixons were Quakers—members of a religious group called the Religious Society of Friends. In his autobiography, Richard Nixon wrote, "Three words described my life in Whittier: family, church, and school."

In his high school, Nixon often spoke on politics and history. He continued that focus when he entered Whittier College in 1930. By the time he graduated, Nixon had decided to study law. He went to Duke University in North Carolina, hoping to join the Federal Bureau of Investigation (FBI) when he graduated. Instead, he returned to California and began working in a small law office. In 1938, Nixon met his future wife, Pat Ryan. They married in 1940.

Washington and the War

At the end of 1941, Nixon accepted a job in Washington, D.C., at the Office of Price Administration (OPA). This organization set limits on the prices charged for certain goods. Before Nixon started the job, the United States entered World War II (1939–1945). After working for the OPA for about six months, Nixon decided to enter the U.S. Navy, which was looking for lawyers and other educated men to serve as officers. After receiving his training, Nixon served as a lieutenant on several islands in the South Pacific.

In 1944, Nixon returned to California. The next year, several business leaders in Whittier suggested that he run for the U.S. House of Representatives for their district. After he was discharged from the navy in 1946, Nixon began his first political campaign.

His Democratic opponent, Jerry Voorhis, had served in Congress for ten years. Nixon, a strong opponent of Communism, suggested that Voorhis had ties to groups that supported Communism. Although not true, these suggestions were a powerful tool for winning votes. The Cold War had already begun, and many Americans were afraid of anyone who seemed connected to Communism.

Nixon won his race, and in 1947, he returned to Washington as a U.S. representative. He quickly won a seat on the House Un-American Activities Committee (HUAC), where he led an investigation into the alleged spying activities of Alger Hiss, a former government official under President Franklin Roosevelt. Although HUAC did not prove that Hiss had been a Soviet spy before World War II, its investigation did lead to Hiss's conviction for lying to Congress. During the Hiss affair, Nixon began to develop a national reputation as a leading anti-Communist.

Hollywood Investigations

Along with investigating Alger Hiss, HUAC is best known for searching for Communists in the motion picture industry. During the late 1940s and early 1950s, a parade of Hollywood stars came to Washington to give the names of people who were or had once been members of the Communist Party in the United States. Some of the people who refused to appear or give names were jailed or fined. HUAC continued to search for Communists in America until 1969.

Representative Richard Nixon as he leaves the federal courthouse in New York after appearing before a special federal grand jury investigating subversive activities. Nixon became associated with anti-Communist causes during his early tenure in the House of Representatives.

Senate and Vice Presidential Service

In 1950, Nixon ran for the U.S. Senate against Helen Gagahan Douglas. Once again, Nixon made questionable—and sometimes false—charges against his opponent's ties to Communists. Nixon easily won the race, but he also acquired a new nickname from Douglas that his opponents used for the rest of his life: "Tricky Dick."

By this time, China had come under Communist rule, and U.S. troops were trying to prevent a Communist takeover in South Korea. Nixon's strong views against Communism made him a rising star in the Republican Party. In 1952, Dwight Eisenhower, the Republican running for president, chose Nixon as the vice presidential candidate in the upcoming election.

Just a few months after Eisenhower chose him, Nixon faced charges that he had illegally received money from a secret fund set up by California business leaders. Nixon denied the charges, appearing on television to defend himself. Afterward, almost 2 million people sent telegrams saying that Nixon should remain as the vice presidential candidate. Eisenhower agreed, although he had not shown much support for Nixon in the controversy.

Eisenhower and Nixon easily won the 1952 election. As vice president, Nixon kept up his attacks on Communism. He also traveled around the globe, representing the U.S. government in about sixty countries. His first trip was to Asia, a part of the world that Eisenhower had never visited. America had an interest in protecting Japan and had just finished fighting in Korea. U.S. leaders also feared the spread of Communism in Southeast Asia. Vietnamese Communists were fighting for their country's independence from France, which they achieved in 1954. From then on, the United States supported anti-Communist forces in the southern part of the country.

One of Nixon's scarier moments abroad came in 1958. The United States, through its large corporations, had

FAST FACT

In his 1952 television speech, Richard Nixon admitted that he and his family had received one personal gift from supporters—a dog named Checkers. Nixon insisted that no matter what anyone said, the family was keeping the dog. His appearance that night was later called "the Checkers speech."

Richard Nixon uses the back of his car as a podium during his campaign for the U.S. Senate in 1950.

great influence over many of the countries in South America. The U.S. government supported South American leaders who tended to be anti-Communist and welcomed U.S. businesses, even though these leaders limited democracy in their countries. These policies led some South Americans to oppose the U.S. government.

In Lima, the capital of Peru, a group of students and Communists shouted "Nixon, go home," and "Death to Nixon." Later, protesters pelted him with fruit, bottles, and rocks. The crowd reaction was even more violent in Caracas, Venezuela. As Nixon drove through the city, rocks splintered the car's windows. When the car stopped, the crowd began rocking it, trying to tip it over. Finally, Nixon's car was able to follow a truck that cut a path through the mob. When he returned home Nixon was treated as a hero.

The next year, Nixon made a trip to Moscow, the capital of the Soviet Union. He was the most important U.S. leader to visit Moscow since the start of the Cold War. Nixon spent a good deal of time with Soviet leader Nikita

Soviet premier Nikita Khrushchev (center left) and American vice president Richard Nixon carry on their famous "kitchen debate" about the merits of the Soviet Communist system versus free enterprise in the United States.

Khrushchev. The two men argued about the merits of their countries and whether Soviet Communism or American free enterprise led to better lives for their citizens. Nixon and Khrushchev visited a fair featuring the latest products from the United States. Standing in a model of a typical U.S. kitchen, they continued their argument, while news cameras recorded the scene. Later, the discussion was called "the kitchen debate." Nixon won praise for standing up to Khrushchev and promoting American values.

Presidential Politics

As vice president, Nixon did not always agree with the president. When Eisenhower accepted a treaty that ended the Korean War (1950–1953), Nixon was willing to keep fighting to win a clear victory over the Communists. He also wanted to spend more money on defense than Eisenhower did. Yet Nixon was loyal to Eisenhower, and that loyalty and his experience earned him the chance to run as the Republican Party's presidential candidate in 1960. In that election he lost a close race to John F. Kennedy.

Nixon went home to California to practice law. In 1962, he ran for governor in California. The campaign was ugly. Nixon and his opponent, Democratic governor Pat Brown, accused each other of illegal campaign practices. When Nixon lost the race, he showed anger toward Brown and the reporters who had covered the campaign, saying, "You won't have Nixon to kick around anymore."

After that speech, both his friends and his enemies thought that Nixon would never run for political office again. However, by 1967, he had won new support from Republican Party leaders, and the next January, he announced his decision to run for president. His opponent that November was Vice President Hubert H. Humphrey. Nixon, claiming that he could achieve "peace with honor" in Vietnam, beat Humphrey in a close race.

A New Vision for Foreign Policy

In Vietnam, Nixon wanted to use U.S. military power in a more decisive way. He also wanted to speed up the process of training and supplying South Vietnamese troops so that they could do more of the fighting. Finally, Nixon wanted to establish better relations with China and the Soviet Union. He hoped that they could pressure their allies in North Vietnam to end the war.

Nixon also thought that Johnson had spent too much time focusing on Southeast Asia. Nixon wanted the United States to pursue closer relations with the other members of the North Atlantic Treaty Organization (NATO), a U.S.-led military alliance. He also said that the country had to play a more active role in the Middle East.

To help carry out his policies, Nixon turned to Henry Kissinger, naming him head of the National Security Council (NSC). This government agency had been created after the start of the Cold War. It helped the president deal with military threats and other foreign issues that affected the country's security.

President Nixon visited U.S. forces in South Vietnam in July 1969. Here he greets combat soldiers from the First Infantry at their headquarters near Di An.

In Vietnam, Nixon made plans to bring home U.S. troops while preparing South Vietnamese forces for battle. Nixon and his advisers called this process "Vietnamization." At the same time, he increased bombing raids over North Vietnam and began secretly bombing enemy forces in neighboring Cambodia, as well. When news of the Cambodia bombing leaked out, young American protesters once again took to the streets, just as they had done in the first years of the war.

By the end of 1969, about 100,000 U.S. troops had returned from Vietnam—yet American ground forces were just about to begin fighting in Cambodia for the first time. Destroying Vietcong bases in Cambodia, Nixon argued, would make it easier to bring home more U.S. troops. This new activity in Southeast Asia led to even more protests.

Talking to the Communists

In August 1969, Kissinger met secretly with North Vietnamese leaders in Paris, France. Peace talks continued off and on for the next several years. The United States also made contact with Chinese and Soviet officials. Some meetings were public, such as the Strategic Arms Limitation Talks (SALT) held in Helsinki, Finland, in November 1969. These talks addressed limiting the number of nuclear weapons built by the United States and the Soviet Union. Other times, however, Nixon and Kissinger used what was called "the back channel." Officials met in private or talked by sending messages through diplomats from other countries. In 1970, for example, the United States made contact with China by sending word through Polish officials.

The U.S. strategy of moving closer to China was sometimes called "playing the China card." The Soviet Union and China had once been allies, but their friendship had weakened. Several times, their troops fought briefly along their shared border, and the Soviet Union moved nuclear weapons and more troops toward the border. Nixon and Kissinger thought that China might want better relations with the United States, since it faced a threat from the Soviet Union. At the same time, they thought that the Soviets might want to improve relations with the United States to prevent a stronger U.S.-Chinese relationship.

For several years, Kissinger talked with Soviet and Chinese officials. This effort to improve relations with the Communists was called *détente*. Nixon saw the value of reducing tensions with the Soviets and Chinese, and since he was such a strong anti-Communist, Americans would not think he had given up on keeping Communism out of the United States.

At the same time, Nixon did not soften his methods for fighting the Vietnam War. He sometimes followed what was called "the madman theory." He wanted the

FAST FACT

California governor Pat Brown was the father of Jerry Brown, who also served as governor of California and three times ran for the Democratic presidential nomination—in 1976, 1980, and 1992.

Communist nations to think that he would do anything—perhaps even use nuclear weapons—to make them back down or give him what he wanted.

Highs and Lows in 1972

In February 1972, Nixon became the first U.S. president to visit Communist China. He met with China's two major leaders, Mao Zedong and Zhou Enlai. Nixon told them that "what is important is not a nation's internal political philosophy. What is important is its policy toward the rest of the world and toward us."

Three months later, Nixon made another historic trip, visiting the Soviet Union. After some difficult discussions, the SALT meetings had finally produced results. In Moscow, Nixon and Soviet leader Leonid Brezhnev signed a treaty that limited the use and development of some weapons. Even with the limits, however, each country still had thousands of nuclear weapons. The two countries could also develop new weapons. The United States and the Soviet Union began a second round of talks, SALT II, later that year. They also tried to improve their economic relations—the Americans sold wheat to the Soviet Union.

Despite the improved ties with China and the Soviet Union, the United States still faced a difficult time in Vietnam. U.S. bombing increased after North Vietnam launched a major attack in the south. After a brief break in the bombing in the fall, Nixon ordered massive bombing raids on North Vietnam in December 1972. These "Christmas bombings," along with pressure from China and the Soviet Union, finally convinced North Vietnam to seek peace. At the same time, Nixon and Kissinger pressured the South Vietnamese to accept a treaty ending the U.S. role in the war.

In January 1973, the United States and the two Vietnams signed a peace treaty. U.S. forces left Vietnam,

though Communists in South Vietnam continued to fight their government, while North Vietnam made major contributions to this effort. To get the South Vietnamese to accept the peace treaty, Nixon had promised to send them money and military supplies. Congress, however, did not spend all the money that Nixon wanted. The war had already cost the United States $150 billion. Some Americans did not want to spend much more in Vietnam.

By this time, Nixon had been reelected president. He easily defeated his Democratic challenger, Senator George McGovern of South Dakota. During the election, however, Nixon faced some questions about the Republican Party's role in a burglary at the Watergate building complex in Washington, D.C. Watergate, as the incident was called, did not harm the president in 1972, but, eventually, Watergate doomed Nixon's presidency.

President Nixon (right) shakes hands with Mao Zedong (left), chairman of the Chinese Communist Party, during a visit to China in 1972. Nixon was the first American president to visit the People's Republic of China.

New Global Concerns

As the U.S. role in Vietnam wound down, Nixon and Kissinger saw problems in other parts of the world. In 1970, voters in Chile had elected Salvador Allende as their president. U.S. officials did not like Allende because he was a *socialist*—he favored government-owned businesses. Nixon used the Central Intelligence Agency (CIA) to try to force Allende from power. In 1973, Chilean military leaders who supported the United States took over the government, and Allende was killed during the fighting. There is no proof that the CIA took part in the attack on Allende. Still, U.S. support for Chile's undemocratic military leaders led many South Americans to criticize the United States.

New troubles also erupted in the Middle East. Since the late 1950s, the United States had supported Israel, which faced the threat of attack from neighboring Arab states. The Soviet Union strongly backed two of Israel's enemies, Egypt and Syria. Another source of tension was

Israeli tanks roll past the remains of Syrian units on the Golan Heights during the Yom Kippur War in 1973.

the Palestinian issue. Arab Palestinians and Jews had both claimed the same territory as their homeland. By the early 1970s, Palestinians in the Middle East were demanding their own country and the elimination of Israel.

In October 1973, Syria and Egypt attacked Israel. The fighting began around the time of the Jewish holy day Yom Kippur, and the battle was called the Yom Kippur War. The war had ties to the Cold War, since the Soviet Union and the United States backed opposing sides.

The Yom Kippur War featured the world's largest tank battle since World War II, which Israel won. After this battle, Kissinger and Brezhnev convinced the two sides to stop fighting. This cease-fire, however, did not last, as the Israelis began the war again. After a second cease-fire, Brezhnev claimed that the Israelis were still fighting. He wanted to send U.S. and Soviet troops to the region to keep the peace. If the Americans did not act, Brezhnev said he would send in troops on his own. Nixon responded by putting U.S. military forces on a high alert. This step let the Soviet Union know that the Americans were ready to fight if Soviet forces went to the Middle East alone. Nixon wrote Brezhnev a note saying that the two nations should act "in harmony and with cool heads." The Soviet Union backed down, and the United Nations (UN) eventually sent in troops to keep the peace.

Watergate Woes

By 1974, Kissinger was handling most of Nixon's foreign affairs. The year before, the president had made Kissinger secretary of state (while he still remained as head of the NSC). Kissinger continued to meet with the Soviet Union, working toward more limits on nuclear weapons.

Nixon's attention had turned away from foreign policy because of the growing Watergate scandal. During 1973, Congress began to investigate the burglary at the

Table Tennis Talks

U.S.-Chinese relations showed signs of improvement in 1971. That year, a U.S. table tennis team went to China to play in a tournament. It was the first time that Americans had made an official visit to China in many years. The trip was sometimes called "ping-pong diplomacy."

SALT Results

In the first SALT treaty, the United States and the Soviet Union agreed to

- limit the use of antiballistic missiles (ABMs)—missiles designed to destroy incoming nuclear missiles—with each country having only two ABM sites

- freeze their number of ICBMs

- freeze their number of nuclear missiles that could be launched from submarines

Vice Presidential Problems

While dealing with Watergate, President Richard Nixon also faced problems with his vice president, Spiro Agnew. Before coming to Washington, D.C., Agnew had been governor of Maryland. In 1973, he was accused of illegally taking money while in Maryland in return for doing favors for certain companies. To avoid a trial, Agnew resigned as vice president in October.

Watergate complex. In June 1972, five men had been caught entering the offices of the National Democratic Party. The burglars wanted to steal information about the Democrats' plans for the upcoming election.

Congress learned that Nixon's advisers had approved the burglary. Nixon had tried to cover up the break-in and the role that his advisers had played in it. The Watergate affair showed that Nixon was willing to lie and break the law to make sure that he was reelected.

Hearings in Congress also revealed that Nixon secretly tape-recorded conversations held in his office. (Every president since Truman had recorded some of his private conversations.) The president went to court to fight Congress's demand to hear all the tapes. Finally, in July 1974, the U.S. Supreme Court ruled that Nixon had to turn over the tapes. By this time, the House of Representatives was preparing to impeach the president. Nixon knew that the tapes would show that he was guilty of lying and trying to cover up the break-in. On August 8, he became the first U.S. president to resign.

During his presidency, Nixon showed that he could be a world leader, taking bold steps to improve America's position in the world. However, his failures in other areas left a black mark on his reputation.

Gerald Ford

THIRTY-EIGHTH PRESIDENT

FACT FILE

NAME
Gerald Rudolph Ford

DATE OF BIRTH
July 14, 1913

PLACE OF BIRTH
Omaha, Nebraska

POLITICAL PARTY
Republican

VICE PRESIDENT
Nelson Rockefeller

SECRETARY OF STATE
Henry Kissinger

YEARS AS PRESIDENT
1974–1977

★ ★ ★

An Unexpected President

Gerald Ford became president during one of the worst political crises in U.S. history. He was picked to serve as vice president in 1973, after the resignation of Spiro Agnew. The next year, Ford stepped up to the presidency after the Watergate scandal forced Richard Nixon to resign. Ford is the only president to reach that office without receiving a vote in a national election.

As a member of the U.S. House of Representatives, Ford was considered honest and hardworking. He seemed a good choice to lead the country after the alleged crimes of President Nixon. However, Ford lacked experience in running a government, and he often fought with Congress, which was controlled by the Democratic Party. In foreign affairs, he faced the same major issues that Nixon had addressed: improving relations with the Soviet Union and aiding anti-Communists in Southeast Asia.

Sports and Law

Gerald Ford was first known as Leslie King. A few years after Leslie was born, his mother divorced his father, an abusive alcoholic. She was soon married again, to a salesman named Gerald R. Ford. She renamed her son after his new stepfather.

Growing up in Grand Rapids, Michigan, Gerald's family was not wealthy, and he held part-time jobs as he went through high school. When he entered the University of Michigan in 1931, he received a football scholarship that paid some of his expenses.

After leaving the University of Michigan, Gerald Ford became a football coach in order to pay his law school expenses.

After his senior year at Michigan, two professional football teams offered Ford jobs, but he wanted to study law. To pay for law school, he took a job coaching football at Yale University in Connecticut. Ford graduated in January 1941 and returned to Michigan to practice law.

From the Navy to the Congress

Soon after the United States entered World War II (1939–1945), Ford joined the navy. He spent more than a year at sea aboard an aircraft carrier. When he left the navy in 1946, he had reached the rank of lieutenant commander. The war changed his opinion about the role of the United States in world affairs. Before joining the navy, he had been an *isolationist*—he thought that America should limit its involvement with other countries. After, he wrote, "The U.S., I was convinced, could no longer stick its head in the sand like an ostrich." To play a more active role in foreign affairs, he believed, the country needed a strong military.

Returning to Grand Rapids, Ford began practicing law again. He also started dating Betty Warren, and they married in October 1948. By then, Ford was running for his first political office—the U.S. House of Representatives. Ford went on to beat the Democratic candidate in November to win the seat in Congress.

In foreign affairs, Ford supported the Marshall Plan, which helped the countries of Western Europe rebuild after World War II. He also backed spending money on defense. Ford sat on the House Appropriations Committee, which plays a large role in deciding how federal money is spent. He also sat on a smaller subcommittee that handled funding of the Central Intelligence Agency (CIA). In domestic affairs, Ford tended to be conservative, trying to limit government spending and opposing laws that reduced the powers of the states.

✔ FAST FACT

Growing up in Grand Rapids, Michigan, Gerald Ford belonged to the Boy Scouts, earning the rank of Eagle Scout. Ford is the only U.S. president who achieved that honor as a Scout.

In 1952, Ford was one of several Republican representatives to ask Dwight Eisenhower to run for president. Ford also approved of Eisenhower's choice for a vice presidential candidate: Richard Nixon. Ford had become friends with Nixon when they served together in the House of Representatives.

Gaining National Attention

The year that Eisenhower was elected, Ford turned down a chance to run for the U.S. Senate. He wanted to remain in the House and perhaps someday become Speaker, the highest position in the House. For most of his time in Congress, however, the Democrats controlled the House, so they chose the Speaker. Ford never had the chance to seek that position. In 1963, he was elected chairman of the House Republican Conference. This group met outside of Congress to decide the party's strategy for passing laws and confronting the Democrats.

Ford won a more powerful position in 1965 when the Republicans named him their leader within the House of Representatives. He actively opposed many of President

House minority leader Gerald Ford listens to Richard Nixon discuss his plans for seeking the Republican nomination for president in 1968. Nixon later asked Ford to join him as the vice presidential candidate. However, Ford declined.

Lyndon Johnson's Great Society programs to aid the poor. He also attacked Johnson's handling of the Vietnam War (1964–1975).

In 1968, Richard Nixon was chosen as the Republican Party's candidate for president. He asked Ford if he was interested in running as his vice president. Ford, however, was still intent on becoming Speaker of the House, so he declined. Nixon then chose Maryland governor Spiro Agnew and went on to win the election.

In June 1972, Ford traveled to China, just months after Nixon became the first U.S. president to visit that Communist country. Ford and Chinese leader Zhou Enlai discussed U.S.-Chinese relations. Zhou stressed that the United States had to keep a strong military to compete with the Soviet Union.

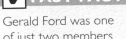

FAST FACT

Gerald Ford was one of just two members of the House of Representatives to serve on the Warren Commission, which investigated the shooting of President John F. Kennedy.

* * *

Watergate and the Vice Presidency

In June 1972, Ford and the rest of the country learned about the break-in at the Watergate building. Five men were caught as they tried to enter the offices of the National Democratic Party. Ford knew that one of the men arrested had ties to President Nixon. He told a friend, "Nixon ought to get to the bottom of this and get rid of anybody who's involved in it." Instead, Nixon and his aides claimed that they had no ties to the burglars and tried to cover up their relations with the arrested men.

Then in September 1973, Vice President Agnew was accused of having taken bribes while governor of Maryland. The next month, after Agnew resigned, Nixon asked Ford to take over. Ford agreed, and on December 6, 1973, he was sworn in as vice president.

Although Ford tried to defend the president, the evidence against Nixon slowly grew. Ford felt trapped. As vice president, he had to be as loyal as possible to the president—an old friend. Yet he did not want to be

FAST FACT

As his vice president, Gerald Ford chose Governor Nelson Rockefeller of New York. He and Ford were the only U.S. vice president and president to serve at the same time without having been elected to their positions.

The oil embargo of 1973–1974 caused long gas lines when service stations threatened to shut down to protest government restrictions on the price they could charge. In this 1973 photo, the price of gas at this California gas station is 36.6 cents per gallon.

"sucked into the whirlpool," as he later wrote. By early August, Ford realized that Nixon had lied to him and the country about his role in Watergate. On August 8, 1974, Nixon resigned, and the next day, Ford was sworn in as president.

Early Problems

Ford's first job was to try to rebuild Americans' faith in their government. He hurt his image, however, with one of his first moves as president. On September 8, Ford granted Nixon a pardon for any crimes that he might have committed as president. Ford was accused of having worked out a deal—Nixon had named him vice president and resigned in return for the pardon. Ford insisted that there was no deal. He said that he pardoned Nixon so that the country could move beyond Watergate and focus on other issues.

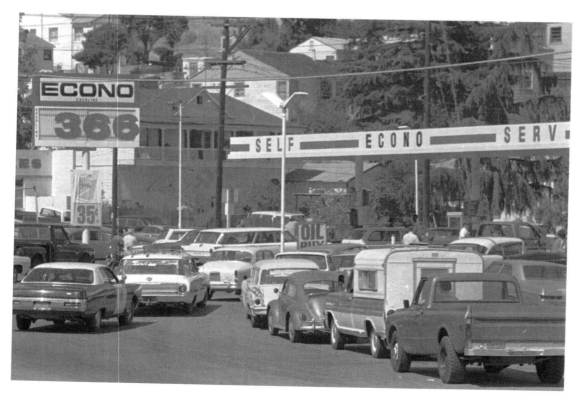

One crucial issue was the struggling economy. Prices were rising at the same time that companies were laying off workers. Some of the problems came from the rising cost of oil, which had its roots in U.S. foreign policy. Starting in November 1973, Arab states had stopped shipping oil to the United States and limited their shipments to other countries. This action, called an *embargo,* was a protest against U.S. support for Israel. Even after the embargo ended in March 1974, prices remained high. Ford urged the country to use less foreign oil. He eventually raised the *tariff*—a kind of tax—on every barrel of foreign oil sold in the country.

Relations with the Soviet Union

Some people questioned Ford's ability to handle foreign relations, but Ford later wrote, "I was confident I knew as much about foreign policy as any member of Congress." He was familiar with defense issues from serving on the Appropriations Committee, and he had traveled overseas. He also could draw on the expertise of Henry Kissinger, who remained as the secretary of state and head of the National Security Council (NSC).

In November 1974, Ford and Kissinger traveled to the Soviet Union to continue the second round of the Strategic Arms Limitation Talks (SALT II), designed to limit nuclear weapons. SALT I, signed in 1972, was going to expire in 1977. Ford and Soviet leader Leonid Brezhnev agreed that each country would have no more than 2,400 ballistic missiles. The two sides also placed limits on some long-range missiles. Each country also asked the other to stop developing certain new weapons, but they could not reach an agreement on this issue. They promised to discuss the matter again at future talks.

At the end of the meeting, both leaders felt that they had taken steps toward preventing a nuclear war. However, in the United States, some politicians did not like Ford's

Cooperation in Space

The summer of 1975 saw an important joint project between the United States and the Soviet Union. About 140 miles (224 kilometers) above Earth, a U.S. *Apollo* spacecraft docked with a Soviet spacecraft called *Soyuz*. Astronauts from the two countries exchanged greetings and gifts. This Apollo-Soyuz Test Project was part of the first SALT agreement. It did not lead to important scientific breakthroughs, but the meeting was a visible sign that the Cold War enemies could work together in the name of détente. The Apollo-Soyuz Test Project was designed to test equipment and methods for rescuing astronauts from damaged spacecraft. The project was the first time that astronauts from different countries worked together in space.

President Ford (center) shakes hands with Soviet general secretary Leonid Brezhnev during the first round of SALT II talks in Helsinki, Finland, in July 1975.

pursuit of *détente*, the policy of improving relations with the Soviet Union. They believed that the U.S. government should not deal with the Soviets as long as they continued to deny the rights of Soviet citizens. Senator Henry "Scoop" Jackson, a Democrat from Washington, was especially concerned about Soviet *dissidents*—people who opposed their Communist government. Jackson led the effort to force the Soviet Union to address human rights issues. Only then, he argued, should the United States deal with the Soviets.

Despite the criticism, Ford pushed for SALT II. He also welcomed the Helsinki Accords, which addressed human rights. During the summer of 1975, representatives from thirty-five nations, including the United States and the Soviet Union, met in Helsinki, the capital of Finland. They signed an agreement with three main sections. The countries agreed to accept the existing borders in Europe, promote trade and the exchange of art and science, and allow the free expression of ideas and free movement by their citizens.

Détente, however, had its limits. Ford still wanted to halt the spread of Soviet influence around the world. Africa became a new setting for Cold War conflicts. Angola, on the west coast of Africa, won its independence from Portugal in 1975. Rival political groups then fought each other, trying to seize power. The United States backed two anti-Communist groups. Congress refused to send direct aid, fearing that the conflict would turn into another Vietnam. Instead, Ford secretly sent arms and supplies. The Soviet Union and Cuba supplied the Angolan Communists, and the Cubans also sent troops. The fighting between rival groups in Angola continued for more than twenty-five years.

Lingering Issues in Southeast Asia

Although U.S. troops left Vietnam in 1973, the United States still supported South Vietnam in its war against Communism. President Nixon had promised the South Vietnamese government billions of dollars in aid. Just a few days after he became president, Ford said, "To our allies and friends in Asia, I pledge continuity in our support for their security, independence, and economic development." Congress, however, had other ideas. It cut requests in military aid for South Vietnam. One reason was the weak U.S. economy; the other was that many Americans were tired of any U.S. role in Vietnam.

Without U.S. aid, the South Vietnamese could not fight the Communists for long. On April 30, 1975, North Vietnam took control of Saigon, the capital in the south, as the last Americans there fled the city. Neighboring Cambodia and Laos also came under Communist control. The final verdict seemed to be in: the United States had lost its war to stop the spread of Communism in Southeast Asia.

A new problem soon emerged in Southeast Asia. On May 12, Cambodian naval boats attacked and captured the *Mayaguez,* a U.S. ship carrying paints, food, and chemicals. Ford first demanded the release of the ship's crew. The diplomatic contact had to be made through the Chinese,

FAMOUS FIGURES

Leonid Brezhnev (1906–1982)

Leonid Brezhnev was one of several top Soviet leaders who forced Nikita Khrushchev to step down in 1964. Brezhnev then became the head of the Soviet Communist Party, the most powerful position in the Soviet Union. Under Brezhnev, the Soviets built more weapons, trying to equal American forces. At the same time, the Soviet leader saw the value of détente. The United States and the Soviets enjoyed their closest relationship since World War II while Brezhnev was in control, but by the end of the 1970s, the Cold War had deepened once again.

Communists in Cambodia

The Communist government of Cambodia during the *Mayaguez* incident was called the *Khmer Rouge*. Khmer is the name of an ancient Cambodian people, and rouge is French for "red." While in power, the *Khmer Rouge* brutally murdered as many as 2 million Cambodians seen as enemies of the state. The events in Cambodia after the Vietnam War were the subject of a 1984 film, *The Killing Fields*.

since the United States did not have direct ties with the new Communist government in Cambodia. The Chinese, however, refused to get involved. In the meantime, U.S. warships steamed to the region.

On May 14, U.S. Marines landed on the island where the ship was docked and the crew was thought to be held. U.S. planes also attacked the Cambodian mainland. While the fighting was going on, the Cambodians released the American prisoners, who were not on the island that the marines attacked. Forty-one Americans died in the effort to free the prisoners.

A Short Stay

The *Mayaguez* incident pleased Americans who did not want the country to seem weak. Most Americans, however, remained more concerned about the economy. Early in 1975, unemployment hit 9 percent, and prices of many goods were still rising. Ford called for a large tax cut and tried to reduce government spending. Congress, however, opposed him and spent more money than he wanted on some programs.

In the 1976 election, Ford hoped to win a full term as president. His opponent was Jimmy Carter, the former governor of Georgia. Carter was not well known, but many voters did not like Ford and his policies. Some were still angry that he had pardoned Richard Nixon. Others thought that he was not smart enough to be president. Ford did not help his chances during the campaign. In a debate with Carter, the president said that the Soviet Union did not dominate the nations of Eastern Europe. That idea seemed ridiculous to many people, since Communist governments tied to the Soviet Union ruled throughout the region. Ford lost the election, ending what had been a sometimes difficult presidency. Still, he had achieved some success in pursuing détente, thanks to the progress that Nixon and Kissinger had made before he took office.

Jimmy Carter

THIRTY-NINTH PRESIDENT

FACT FILE

NAME
James Earl Carter

DATE OF BIRTH
October 1, 1924

PLACE OF BIRTH
Plains, Georgia

POLITICAL PARTY
Democratic

VICE PRESIDENT
Walter Mondale

SECRETARIES OF STATE
Cyrus Vance (1977–1980)
Edmund Muskie (1980–1981)

YEARS AS PRESIDENT
1977–1981

An Unknown Politician

Few Americans had heard of Jimmy Carter when he first announced that he was running for president. Carter's only major political position had been governor of Georgia. Still, in 1976, Americans were ready for a fresh political face after the painful years of the Vietnam War (1964–1975) and Watergate. Carter defeated Gerald Ford to become the thirty-ninth president of the United States.

In foreign affairs, Carter promised to promote human rights. During the Cold War, Carter believed, the United States had supported dictators just because they opposed Communism. Carter wanted to end this practice while continuing to pursue *détente,* the policy of improving relations with the Soviet Union. As president, however, Carter found it hard to achieve his goals. His presidency ended with a foreign relations disaster: the kidnapping of Americans in Iran.

A Farm Boy in the Navy

Jimmy Carter's parents, Earl and Lillian, owned farms in Plains, Georgia, where they raised peanuts, cotton, and other crops. They also owned a warehouse and a country store. Earl Carter held several public offices, including a seat in the Georgia state legislature.

As a boy, Carter worked hard on the farm and in school. At eleven, he entered the Baptist Church, and his religion has remained important to him throughout his life. Carter decided that he wanted to join the navy and he made plans to attend the U.S. Naval Academy even before entering high school.

Carter entered the academy, located in Annapolis, Maryland, in 1943. By then, the United States was heavily involved in World War II (1939–1945). Carter never saw action—he did not graduate from Annapolis until 1946. He left school with the rank of ensign and became an instructor on a U.S. battleship. By this time, he had married Rosalynn Smith, and their first child was born in 1947.

Lieutenant Jimmy Carter (center standing) is shown observing instruments aboard the submarine USS K-1 in 1952.

Submarine Service

After two years on battleships, Carter entered the navy's submarine service. This introduced him to an important new technology: nuclear energy. At the end of World War II, the United States had used the tremendous energy stored in the atoms of radioactive materials to create a nuclear bomb. Scientists also saw that this energy could be controlled and used to power submarines and create electricity at power plants. During the early 1950s, the U.S. Navy began building submarines that used nuclear power. These subs could stay underwater for months at a time without refueling. Nuclear subs became an important new weapon in the Cold War. U.S. subs patrolled the waters off the Soviet Union, ready to launch nuclear missiles at a moment's notice.

Carter never served on a nuclear sub. In 1953, his father died, and Carter decided to leave the navy and return to Plains. Because of his father's ill health, the family farm had started to fail. Carter hoped to make it profitable again.

Nuclear Navy

In the U.S. Navy, Admiral Hyman Rickover led the effort to build nuclear submarines. Jimmy Carter worked closely with Rickover and called him one of the most important people in his life. Rickover's work led to the launching of the USS *Nautilus,* the world's first nuclear sub, in 1954. Rickover wanted even more ships to run on nuclear power. Today, almost all U.S. subs and most large aircraft carriers use nuclear power as their fuel.

Georgia Politics

Life on the farm was not easy. Over time, however, Carter learned new farming techniques. His skill and hard work improved the family business. Carter also became active in the local community, serving on the county board of education and the boards of local nonprofit organizations.

In 1962, Carter entered his first political race for a seat in the Georgia state senate. He had to run in a primary to win the Democratic nomination. Carter lost the primary vote, but he proved in court that his opponent's backers had cast illegal votes. A judge ruled that Carter was the Democratic candidate. That fall, he won the seat in the senate.

Carter won reelection to the senate in 1964. He was already thinking about running for U.S. Congress two years

FAST FACT

As a politician, Jimmy Carter was sometimes called a *populist*—someone who supports the interests of farmers, small business owners, and workers over the interests of large corporations and the wealthy.

later, but at the beginning of 1966 he changed his mind and ran for governor instead. He faced a crowded field, as several other candidates ran for the Democratic nomination. In the primary vote he came in third.

Moving into the National Arena

Four years later, Carter ran for governor again, and this time he won. He stressed protecting the rights of the poor and of working people. He felt that he was someone who "understands their problems, who has worked with his hands, who knows what it means to be left out." He ran what some considered a mean race, attacking his major opponent with half-truths.

As governor Carter acted as a social and political reformer, although he had not discussed reform much as a candidate. He tried to improve the lives of African Americans at a time when many Georgians still held racist views. Carter also tried to help the mentally disabled, protect

Governor Jimmy Carter poses for a photo at his desk at the state capital in Atlanta, Georgia in 1971.

the rights of consumers, and preserve the environment.

When Carter left the governor's office in January 1975, he was already a candidate for the 1976 presidential election, which the Democrats seemed to have a good chance of winning. At the time, the country was still shocked from the Watergate scandal. Republican president Richard Nixon had resigned his office rather than face charges that he broke the law. The new president, Gerald Ford, then pardoned Nixon for any crimes he might have committed.

Many Americans were also disgusted with their leaders after the U.S. loss in the Vietnam War. The goal had been to stop the spread of Communism in Southeast Asia, but by the spring of 1975, all of Vietnam and two neighboring countries were under Communist rule. More than 58,000 Americans had died in the war with nothing good to show for it.

Given the public's mood, Carter thought he would make an excellent candidate. Not having served in Washington during Watergate and Vietnam might seem like a plus to voters. Carter also came across as honest and caring. He won the Democratic nomination that summer, then beat President Ford in the election.

FAST FACT

In 1972, Jimmy Carter received national attention when he spoke at the Democratic Convention, held to choose the party's candidate for president. For some Democratic leaders, the speech was their first chance to see Carter and hear his political ideas.

The Push for Human Rights

Although he did not have experience in foreign affairs, Carter had several clear goals. He wanted to cut defense spending and not send U.S. troops abroad, if possible. He wanted to continue détente with the Soviet Union. Yet he also wanted to make sure that any new deals did not favor the Soviets. Most important, he believed that the United States should promote human rights. He wanted a foreign policy, he said, that was "designed to serve mankind." The United States would end its support of dictators and promote democracy around the world.

In reality, however, Carter found that it was hard to end ties with dictators who supported the United States.

Nicaraguan president
Anastasio Somoza in
military camouflage shortly
before his exile in 1979.
Somoza was one of the
anti-Communist military
leaders who received U.S.
support during the Carter
administration although his
government did not have a
good human rights record.

During his presidency, the country continued to support
leaders that limited democracy, such as the military rulers
of El Salvador, Anastasio Somoza of Nicaragua, and Shah
Mohammed Reza Pahlavi of Iran. The U.S. government
under Carter still saw a need to support some anti-
Communist governments, even if they did not honor
human rights. In other cases, supporting dictators was
important for protecting U.S. business interests.

Carter took a more forceful stand on human rights in
Communist countries. Early in 1977, he became interested
in the case of Soviet scientist Andrei Sakharov. He had
once helped build nuclear weapons for his country but was
later arrested for speaking out against Communism. Carter
sent him a letter promising to address human rights as he
dealt with the Soviet government. Soviet leader Leonid
Brezhnev then sent the president an angry letter telling
Carter to back off on human rights. Brezhnev wrote,
"Washington's claims to teach others how to live cannot be
accepted by any...state."

Carter, however, believed that the United States and
the Soviet Union had "a fundamental difference in
philosophy concerning human freedoms, and it [did] not
benefit us to cover it up." The Carter administration
supported the actions of several human rights groups that
sprang up in Eastern Europe after the Helsinki Accords,
agreements that were supposed to protect human rights.
Anti-Communists in several Eastern European nations set
up what were called Helsinki Watch groups. They kept
track of their governments' actions that limited human
rights. U.S. support did not stop Communist governments
from arresting members of these watch groups.

New Pace to the Arms Race

In one of his first acts as president, Carter suggested that
the United States and the Soviet Union should deeply cut
the number of their nuclear weapons. The Soviets were not
interested. They felt that the two countries already had a
good relationship, established in 1974 between their leader,
Leonid Brezhnev, and President Ford. That agreement
would be the blueprint for the second round of Strategic
Arms Limitation Talks (SALT II). Meetings for SALT II
went on, yet both countries also took steps to modernize
their weapons.

First, the Soviet Union introduced a new missile, the
SS-20. It had a range of about 3,000 miles (4,800
kilometers), making it an intermediate-range missile.
(Long-range missiles could go much farther, traveling from
the Soviet Union to the United States.) The SS-20 alarmed
U.S. allies in Europe, since the missile could carry nuclear
warheads to their countries.

President Carter responded by proposing that the
United States introduce new intermediate-range missiles.
These weapons would be based in Western Europe and
aimed at the Soviet Union. At the same time, the United

President Carter proposed deploying land-based cruise missiles, such as the one in the photo, in Europe in 1979 as a deterrent to the Soviet Union.

States made plans to spend more money on conventional (nonnuclear) weapons. Yet the Carter administration also worked to ease tensions by seeking cuts in nuclear arms. This approach of increasing the size of the military while seeking nuclear cuts was called a "twin track" policy.

The Soviet Union did not welcome the idea of new U.S. missiles in Europe. Even before Carter announced his plan in 1979, Brezhnev accused Carter of trying to bring back the worst of the Cold War. Some of the blame, he said, rested with one of Carter's top advisers, Zbigniew Brzezinski. As Carter's national security adviser, Brzezinski often took a tough stance against Communism and the Soviet Union. Carter began to embrace some of Brzezinski's views. In June 1978, he said, "The Soviet Union can choose either confrontation or cooperation. The United States is adequately prepared for both."

Some Europeans also did not want new U.S. weapons on their soil. In West Germany, hundreds of thousands of people protested the missiles, fearing that their country could become a battle zone for Soviet and U.S. nuclear weapons. Nevertheless, the plan to introduce the missiles went forward.

Cold War Hot Spots

During the Carter presidency, small Cold War conflicts went on around the world. In Angola, Cuban troops continued to play a role in that country's civil war. Cuba and the Soviet Union supported Communist forces there, while the United States backed anti-Communist groups. The Cubans in Angola were also training rebels from neighboring Zaire, who then returned to attack their homeland in 1977 and 1978.

The Soviets and Cubans were also active in eastern Africa in a region called the Horn of Africa. A war developed between two countries on the Horn, Ethiopia and Somalia. The Soviet Union sent supplies to Ethiopia, while Cuba sent 12,000 troops. Brzezinski and Carter were alarmed at the growing Communist involvement on the Horn, but they did not send aid to Somalia.

Cuba also had an interest in aiding Communists in Latin America. In 1979, a rebellion broke out in Nicaragua. For decades, the family of Anastasio Somoza had ruled that country. They used the military to control the population while taking most of the country's wealth for themselves. According to Carter's human rights policy, the United States should have ended support for Somoza. Instead, the president hoped to reform Somoza's government while still backing it.

The Nicaraguans who opposed Somoza held different political beliefs. Some wanted democracy. Others, called the Sandinistas, supported Communism. The Sandinistas led the revolution that forced Somoza from power. Then the Sandinistas turned to Cuba for support. They also modeled parts of their government after the one that Fidel Castro had set up in Cuba after his successful revolution in 1959. By the end of Carter's term, most non-Communists had left the Nicaraguan government. The country would become an important Cold War battleground under President Ronald Reagan.

Dueling Advisers

Before serving as national security adviser, Zbigniew Brzezinski taught at Columbia University in New York City. Born in Poland, he disliked that the Soviet Union had placed his homeland under Communist rule. Brzezinski sometimes argued with Carter's other top foreign policy adviser, Secretary of State Cyrus Vance, who had served in the Defense Department during the 1960s. Vance was not as convinced as Brzezinski that the Soviet Union was at the heart of most conflicts around the world.

From the Panama Canal to the Great Wall

President Jimmy Carter (left) shakes hands with General Omar Torrijos, the leader of Panama, after they signed the Panama Canal treaty in 1977. The treaty turned over control of the Panama Canal and the surrounding land from the United States to Panama.

Despite Cold War conflicts Carter did have some successes overseas. For more than ten years, U.S. and Panamanian leaders had been trying to work out a deal that would guarantee U.S. access to the Panama Canal while giving it and the land around it to Panama. In 1977, the two countries finally agreed that the United States would turn over control of the Panama Canal to the Panamanian government.

At home, however, Carter faced harsh criticism for the Panama Canal treaties. The Senate had to approve the deal, and many senators thought that Carter had given up too much. Opponents, calling the agreement a "giveaway,"

demanded that the United States keep the right to send its military to the canal if it ever came under attack. Carter had to work hard to win approval, but the Senate finally passed the treaties regarding the canal in 1978.

The strong opposition to the Panama Canal treaties was the first sign of a growing conservative movement in the United States. In foreign policy, the conservatives wanted to maintain a strong military and to assert the interests of the United States—especially regarding the Cold War.

Conservatives attacked Carter again in 1979, when he announced that the United States would have official diplomatic relations with Communist China. In 1949, anti-Communist Chinese forces, called Nationalists, had set up their own government on the island of Taiwan. The United States had refused to accept the Communist government on the mainland of China as the true Chinese government. In 1972, President Nixon made the first U.S. diplomatic contact with Communist China. Still, the U.S. government continued to recognize the Chinese government in Taiwan as the "real" China. Carter's move in 1979 upset Americans who believed that he should continue to support Taiwan's claim as the legal Chinese government.

However, Carter thought the time was right to have official ties with Communist China. To mark the occasion, Carter and his wife traveled to China and met with its leader, Deng Xiaoping. Carter hoped that the Americans and Chinese could work together to solve international problems. China might help the United States make contact with other nations that did not want to deal directly with Americans. Better relations with China might also pressure the Soviet Union to seek more arms talks with the United States. Carter was playing "the China card," as Nixon and Henry Kissinger had done in the early 1970s. Here, however, Carter's plan backfired a bit. Alarmed by the new relationship between the United States and China, the Soviets became harder to deal with on SALT II. Still, the arms talks went on.

Pulling out of Panama

The Panama Canal treaties said that the United States would turn the Canal Zone over to Panama on December 31, 1999. The treaties also guaranteed that the Canal Zone would always remain neutral during a war; ships from any country could pass through it. If the canal ever were attacked, the United States would join Panama in defending it.

 **FAST FACT**

The Sandinistas were named for Augusto Cesar Sandino, a Nicaraguan military officer who led a rebellion against the U.S. troops that controlled his country during the late 1920s and early 1930s.

A Middle East Success

Carter's greatest diplomatic triumph came in the Middle East. Israel and Egypt had been in a state of war since the founding of Israel in 1948. Egypt, usually with its Arab allies, had fought four wars with Israel losing each time. Relations with the Arabs were also tense because the Palestinians wanted their own country in land controlled by Israel. Lebanon was also a hot spot, as Israel supported Christian Lebanese in a civil war against Muslims. Palestinians and forces from Syria also fought in the war.

In the midst of this violence, Egyptian president Anwar Sadat indicated that he was ready to discuss peace. In 1977, he traveled to Israel to begin a dialogue with the country's leaders. The next year, Carter invited Sadat and Israeli prime minister Menachem Begin to Camp David in Maryland to try to reach an agreement.

Egyptian president Anwar Sadat, U.S. president Jimmy Carter, and Israeli prime minister Menachem Begin sign the Camp David Accords on September 17, 1978.

For almost two weeks, Carter worked with the two foreign leaders and their aides. Finally, Israel and Egypt reached two accords. They would hold future talks to discuss letting Arabs in lands under Israeli control form

their own government. The Palestinians and the government of Jordan would be involved in the process. Begin and Sadat also agreed to declare peace if Israel pulled out of the Sinai, Egyptian land that it had won after the 1967 Six-Day War. In return, Sadat would officially recognize Israel as a nation.

After signing the Camp David Accords, as they were called, Israel and Egypt began working on an official peace treaty. When the talks broke down, Carter flew to the Middle East in March 1979. Once again, he convinced the two sides to reach an agreement. Sadat and Begin signed the peace treaty, ending the hostility between their nations, and the two leaders later won the Nobel Peace Prize. Carter won praise for achieving a great diplomatic victory. Violence, however, did not end in the Middle East, for the Palestinian problem proved difficult to solve.

FAST FACT

Camp David, located in central Maryland, has been a vacation spot for U.S. presidents since the 1930s. The camp also gives presidents a place to meet privately with foreign leaders.

A Middle East Failure

In another part of the Middle East, Carter faced a growing crisis. Revolution had broken out in Iran in 1978, forcing Iranian leader Shah Mohammed Reza Pahlavi to flee his country. (*Shah* is Persian for "king.") The shah had a long relationship with the United States. In part, that relationship fueled the revolution in Iran.

The Pahlavi family had come to power in Iran at the beginning of the twentieth century. They ruled a country prized for its huge reserves of oil. Mohammed Reza Pahlavi came to power in 1941, but in 1953, political opponents seized control. They nationalized the country's oil, meaning that the Iranian government, not a private company, received the profits. The Central Intelligence Agency (CIA) then helped Shah Pahlavi return to power. After that, the CIA helped the shah develop a secret police force, called SAVAK. This agency used violence and terror to prevent Iranians from opposing the shah and his policies.

By the 1970s, Pahlavi was using Iran's oil wealth to modernize the country. The shah also spent billions of dollars to buy weapons—most of them from the United States. U.S. leaders wanted Iran to be strong so that the shah could prevent any kind of Communist threat. His forces could also end any other problem in the region that threatened to stop the flow of oil to the United States.

When he took office, Carter had mixed feelings about Iran. On the one hand, the government denied the human rights of its citizens. Yet Carter saw that the shah helped keep the peace in the region. For a time, Carter cut off arms sales to Iran to force the shah to reform his policies, and Pahlavi did take action. He released some political prisoners and granted more freedom to the press. However, SAVAK continued to operate. Still, Carter welcomed the changes. On December 31, 1977, while visiting the Iranian capital of Tehran, he praised Iran as "an island of stability in one of the more troubled areas of the world."

Despite Carter's optimism, Iran soon had troubles of its own. Some of the shah's strongest enemies were Muslim *fundamentalists*. These Iranians wanted Islamic religious

An effigy of the deposed shah of Iran is burned outside the U.S. embassy in Tehran, Iran, in 1979. Iranians began protesting the shah's rule while he was undergoing medical treatment in the United States at the invitation of President Carter.

leaders to run the government. They closely followed the teachings of the *Qur'an* (known in the West as the *Koran*), the holiest book in the Islamic religion. The fundamentalists also did not like the modern ways of life that the shah had introduced. They blamed him and his supporter—the United States—for reducing the role of Islam in Iranian society.

The top religious leader, or *ayatollah*, of the fundamentalists was Ruholla Khomeini. Khomeini's followers joined other Iranians opposed to the shah to force him out of power. By the beginning of 1979, Khomeini and the fundamentalists were in control and the shah was in Egypt.

The crisis deepened in the fall of 1979, when Carter let the shah come to the United States for medical treatment. On November 4, Iranian students loyal to Khomeini stormed the U.S. embassy in Tehran. They took sixty-six Americans hostage. The Iranians demanded that the United States send the shah back to Iran to face trial and execution. Khomeini said that the students had acted on their own, but he had approved their actions.

Several hostages were later released and a few more escaped, leaving fifty-two Americans hostage. For the rest of his presidency, Carter struggled to win the freedom of the fifty-two Americans. He tried to pressure the Iranians by refusing to buy their oil and denying them access to their money in U.S. banks. He also tried to negotiate secretly with the Iranians. These tactics did not work, and the hostages remained imprisoned.

In the spring of 1980, Carter finally agreed to try to use force to free the hostages. Secretary of State Cyrus Vance opposed the move. Carter ignored Vance's concerns, even though he knew that the rescue mission was risky. On April 24, eight helicopters and six planes carrying soldiers took off from different points, scheduled to meet in the Iranian desert. Bad weather and equipment problems forced the mission to end before the soldiers could reach Tehran. To make matters worse, a plane and a helicopter crashed into each other, killing eight U.S. soldiers.

Ayatollah Ruholla Khomeini (1902–1989)

Ayatollah Ruholla Khomeini was the most visible religious leader of Iran's Shi'ites, one of the two major branches of Islam. In 1963, the shah of Iran arrested Khomeini for protesting the government's close ties with the United States. Khomeini was forced to live abroad for many years, first in Turkey and then in Iraq and France. He returned to Iran to take control of the government created after the fall of the shah in 1979. Khomeini set up a government that put Muslim fundamentalist religious leaders in control. That government continued in Iran after Khomeini's death in 1989.

The Soviet Union on the Attack

As trouble grew in Iran, Carter continued efforts to work out an arms agreement with the Soviet Union. In June 1979, Carter and Brezhnev signed SALT II. The treaty limited the number of each country's long-range missiles and bomber planes. The next step was for the Senate to approve the treaty, but events in Afghanistan ended SALT II.

In 1978, a Communist government that supported the Soviet Union had come to power in Afghanistan. Many Muslims in the country opposed Communism, since it did not allow the free practice of religion. Afghan fundamentalists felt that Communism was a threat to traditional ways—just as Iranian fundamentalists felt threatened by American values. Some fundamentalists began to fight the new Afghan government. They were called *mujahedeen*—"soldiers of god."

Carter sent some basic supplies to help the mujahedeen. The United States wanted to help anti-Communist forces—even if they were not particularly friendly to the United States. Later, Carter asked Pakistan, a neighbor of Afghanistan, to arm and train the mujahedeen. At the same time, the Soviet Union sent aid to the Afghan Communists.

During 1979, the situation in Afghanistan changed. Soviet support for Afghan leader Hazifullah Amin began to weaken as he pursued government policies that the Soviets did not like. Amin then began to consider seeking closer ties with the United States. Soviet leaders decided to invade Afghanistan so that they could install a new government that would follow their orders. On December 24, the first Soviet tanks and soldiers crossed into Afghanistan.

The invasion angered Carter. He said that the move "could pose the most serious threat to the peace since the Second World War." In response, he took several new steps. He withdrew his support for SALT II and announced

that the United States was planning to open new naval bases in the Middle East and eastern Africa. He also cut off grain sales to the Soviet Union and asked Congress to increase defense spending. Finally, he used the CIA to send weapons to the mujahedeen.

FAST FACT

Jimmy Carter joined Theodore Roosevelt and Woodrow Wilson as the only U.S. presidents to win the Nobel Peace Prize.

Painful Last Days

While juggling problems all over the world, Carter also faced problems at home. The Iranian crisis had led to another gas shortage similar to the ones in 1973 and 1974. Prices soared and people had to wait in long lines to fill up their tanks. In general, the economy had worsened since 1977. Inflation was much higher, meaning that the costs of most goods had risen dramatically. More people were out of work than when Carter took office. The Iranian hostage crisis also hurt Carter's image. His failure to free the hostages made him seem ineffective.

In July 1980, a national poll showed that just 21 percent of Americans approved of Carter's performance as president. It was the lowest score that any president had ever received since the poll was first taken in 1936. That rating would make it hard for Carter to win reelection. Carter opposed Republican Ronald Reagan in the November presidential election.

Reagan, a conservative, did not trust the Soviets and vowed to fight the spread of Communism. In public, Reagan often spoke without checking his facts, but he came across as likable and strong. Carter, by contrast, had broken many of the promises that he had made in 1976 and seemed weak. Reagan beat Carter easily.

Before leaving office, Carter and his advisers continued to work for the release of the American hostages in Iran. The United States finally agreed to let Iran take its money held in U.S. banks in return for the hostages' freedom. Carter hoped that he would still be president when the hostages were released. Instead, Iran freed them on January 20, 1981, just minutes after Ronald Reagan was sworn in as president.

As president, Carter had one great diplomatic achievement: the Camp David Accords. However, his failures, especially with Iran, tainted his reputation. He did not achieve any great gains in human rights, as he had promised. Since leaving office, however, Carter has played a role in ending diplomatic disputes in several countries. He has also donated a lot of time and money to charity. In many ways, Carter has won more respect as a former president than he did when he was in the White House. The final proof of that came in 2002, when he won the Nobel Peace Prize. The award honored him for his work at Camp David and his efforts at diplomacy after leaving office.

Iranian demonstrators hold a sign depicting the United States as a warmonger and another showing a mystical portrait of Ayatollah Khomeini during the fourth week of the Iranian hostage crisis.

Ronald Reagan

FORTIETH PRESIDENT

FACT FILE

NAME
Ronald Wilson Reagan

DATE OF BIRTH
February 6, 1911

PLACE OF BIRTH
Tampico, Illinois

POLITICAL PARTY
Republican

VICE PRESIDENT
George Bush

SECRETARIES OF STATE
Alexander Haig Jr. (1981–1982)
George Shultz (1982–1989)

YEARS AS PRESIDENT
1981–1989

★ ★ ★

"The Great Communicator" in Charge

A strong conservative, Ronald Reagan firmly believed in confronting Communism around the world. The former actor used humor and a relaxed speaking style to communicate his deeply held beliefs on the Cold War and other issues. His ideas appealed to Americans who thought that the United States had grown weak after Vietnam, Watergate, and the Iranian hostage crisis.

During his eight years as president, Reagan generated mixed emotions. Conservatives thought that he was a hero who rebuilt America's pride. Liberal critics said that his ideas were too simple for a complex world and gave too much influence to big business. Reagan's greatest achievement was helping to bring an end to the Cold War, but his foreign policy also led to a scandal known as the Iran-Contra affair. Despite the scandal, he remained one of the most popular presidents in modern times.

Growing Up "Dutch"

Ronald Reagan grew up in several small towns in Illinois before settling in Dixon. Regan was known as "Dutch" because his father, Jack, once said that the boy looked like a "fat Dutchman." The Reagans often faced poverty, as Jack Reagan struggled with alcoholism. During the 1930s, he landed a job with a government agency, the Works Progress Administration (WPA). The WPA was part of Franklin Roosevelt's *New Deal*—government programs designed to help Americans suffering from the Great Depression. Like his mother, Nelle, Ronald developed an interest in acting. Nelle Reagan often organized plays and dramatic readings in Dixon.

In high school, Reagan was a good athlete and served as president of the student body. He also performed in plays and wrote for the school yearbook. He kept up his busy schedule at Eureka College, a small school not far from Dixon. Graduating from Eureka in 1932, Reagan took a job at a radio station in Iowa as a sports broadcaster. His speaking skills helped him land a position at a bigger station where he covered major league baseball games and other sports.

Ronald Reagan is ready to start his sports broadcast at radio station WHO in Des Moines, Iowa, in 1937. That year, Reagan won a trip to Hollywood, California, as first prize in a contest for the best baseball broadcaster in the Midwest.

On to Hollywood

In 1937, while visiting California, Reagan made a screen test—a short appearance on film to show his skills. Within a few months, he was living in California and working for one of the major film studios in Hollywood, the center of the film industry.

For the next several years, Reagan was busy in Hollywood making eight or nine pictures a year. He later wrote that film "had brought me star status." His career might have gone even farther if not for World War II (1939–1945). Like many Hollywood stars, Reagan joined the military. Bad eyesight kept him off the battlefield, so he made training films for the U.S. Army Air Force. He also appeared in war films for regular movie audiences.

From Liberal to Conservative

Near the end of the war and just after, Reagan joined several liberal groups, including the American Veterans Committee. He was also actively involved with the Screen Actors Guild (SAG), the union for film actors. Reagan's involvement with the union and political groups began his shift from liberal Democrat to conservative Republican.

During the 1930s, a number of Americans thought that Communism offered a solution to the economic problems that gripped the country. Some of these people went to meetings sponsored by the Communist Party of the United States of America or related groups. Others—including some people working in Hollywood—joined the Communist Party.

Many union members across the country were also interested in Communism. Some Communists were involved in union activities—but so were liberals like Reagan. By the end of World War II, some liberals began to speak out against the Communists. Reagan was one of the first. He quit several

FAST FACT

Ronald Reagan married his first wife, Jane Wyman, in 1940. She later became a major star, winning the 1948 Academy Award for Best Actress. That same year, she and Reagan divorced. Wyman did not like Reagan's growing involvement in politics.

FAST FACT

Besides making light bulbs and household appliances, GE plays a large role in the defense industry. It makes engines for planes and once built and tested nuclear weapons.

groups that he learned had ties to Communists. In 1947, as president of the SAG, he helped lead the effort to remove Communists from the film industry.

These activities came just as the Cold War was developing. Many Americans believed that Communists were trying to destroy the country's political and economic system. Even liberals were under suspicion. Reagan later wrote that "light was dawning in some obscure region of my head"—he was coming to believe that liberal policies were dangerous. Conservatives believed that liberals defended the rights of people, such as Communists, who wanted to harm the United States and that liberals refused to see the threat posed by American Communists, who usually supported the Soviet Union.

Reagan remained president of the SAG until 1952. He continued to speak out forcefully against Communism. He also began to call for cutting taxes. By now, Reagan was a highly paid star. He remained a Democrat, but he supported Republican Dwight Eisenhower for president and developed increasingly conservative views.

Two more events shaped Reagan's conservative attitudes. In 1952, he married his second wife, Nancy Davis. She came from a wealthy and conservative family. Two years later, Reagan became a public speaker for General Electric (GE). He served as host of a TV show that the company sponsored. He also toured the country speaking to business leaders and GE workers. Many of his speeches focused on reducing the role of government in business—a key part of conservative thought. Reagan worked for GE for eight years. In 1962, Reagan joined the Republican Party.

Entry into Politics

In 1964, Reagan strongly supported Senator Barry Goldwater of Arizona, the Republican candidate for president. Most Americans, however, did not welcome the senator's views. His opponent, Lyndon Johnson, suggested that Goldwater was likely to lead the United States into a nuclear war with the Soviet Union.

In late October, some conservative Californians paid for time on national television so that Reagan could speak in support of Goldwater. The speech gave most Americans their first chance to hear Reagan talk on political issues. He called the United States "the last best hope of man on Earth." The speech helped the Republican Party bring in $8 million in donations. It also made Reagan the new hero of the conservative movement.

Just a few months after Reagan made his Goldwater speech, some California business owners suggested that he run for governor of the state. Reagan entered the race in January 1966, trying to win the Republican nomination. His opponent was George Christopher, a moderate Republican. Reagan easily defeated Christopher and then faced Democratic governor Edmund "Pat" Brown Sr. Voters liked Reagan's positive approach and his promise to make California better by reducing the role of the

Ronald Reagan reaches out to supporters of his 1966 campaign to unseat Governor Edmund Brown of California. Reagan won the election and served two terms as governor of the state.

FAST FACT

During his first year as governor of California, Reagan asked for a $1 billion tax increase—the largest single increase ever for a U.S. state.

government. In November, the voters elected Reagan to his first political office.

Reagan tried to put his conservative views into practice, but it was not always easy. He was forced to raise taxes when he entered office, since California's finances were in bad shape. He also usually faced a Democratic legislature that resisted his conservative measures. Still, Reagan did meet some of his goals. He reduced the number of people who received *welfare*—government money that helps the needy pay for living expenses. At the same time, the people who did receive welfare received more money. Reagan also tried to reduce the overall amount of money that the state spent, or at least slow the rate at which government spending increased.

Reagan took a firm stand against student protesters at California's universities. On some occasions, he used the National Guard to keep schools open when protesters tried to shut them down. This tough step made Reagan popular with voters. His policies also improved the state's economy. In 1970, Reagan won a second term as governor.

Eyeing the White House

In 1968, Reagan made a brief attempt to seek the Republican presidential nomination. When he stepped down as governor of California in 1974, he was already planning a more serious run for his party's nomination in the 1976 elections. By the end of 1975, he officially announced that he would challenge President Gerald Ford for the Republican nomination.

Reagan scared away some voters with his economic plans. One plan would have cut federal income taxes but forced states to raise their taxes to pay for programs such as welfare. Reagan seemed to do better discussing foreign policy. He attacked Ford and Richard Nixon for seeking arms talks with the Soviet Union. He also criticized ongoing talks to turn over control of the Panama Canal from the United States to the government of Panama. "We bought it," he told one audience, "we paid for it, it's ours, and we aren't going to give it away."

Conservative crowds loved Reagan's tough talk, but he could not win enough votes to claim the nomination. Reagan stayed in the public eye. He again made daily radio broadcasts, speaking on domestic and foreign affairs. At home, he advocated federal tax cuts, fewer laws restricting businesses, and cuts in welfare spending. He also promoted the role of religion and what were later called "family values." Reagan did not want to protect the legal rights of homosexuals, calling homosexuality "a tragic illness."

In foreign affairs, Reagan continued to warn about the danger of Communism. He opposed dealing with the Soviet Union on any level. "I wouldn't trust the Russians…they must be laughing at us because we continue to think of them as people like us." He also worried about Cuba and China spreading Communism and threatening U.S. interests.

Reagan believed that some Americans aided the goals of the Communists by joining groups that called for arms reductions. Reagan rightfully claimed that at least one peace group active in the United States had ties to the Soviet Union. Yet he then suggested that Americans who belonged to other peace groups were somehow tied to the Soviet-backed group. Reagan claimed that the effort by some Americans to limit nuclear power could also be traced to the Soviet Union.

In 1980, Reagan won the Republican presidential nomination. During the campaign, President Carter tried to show that Reagan was too extreme in his views. Voters, however, supported Reagan's call for a larger military, federal tax cuts, and a smaller role for the national government. Carter was hurt by the weak economic conditions and the Iranian hostage crisis. In November, Reagan easily beat Carter.

FAST FACT

One policy that Ronald Reagan opposed before 1980 was selling U.S. grain to the Soviet Union. As president, however, Reagan allowed the sales in order to increase income for U.S. farmers.

Attack on the President

On March 30, 1981, an assassin named John Hinckley shot and wounded President Reagan. He also wounded three other people, including Reagan aide Jim Brady. Despite the attack, Reagan remained in his usual good spirits and quickly recovered from his injury.

The Reagan Revolution

As in California, Reagan's aides played a large role in working out the details of his administration's plans. President Reagan was most comfortable speaking about the general ideas of his conservative policies. At home, he pushed for the tax cuts that he had always wanted and tried to reduce spending on some social programs. His approach was sometimes called "Reaganomics" or "the Reagan Revolution."

Reagan moved quickly to spend billions of dollars more on defense. The funds were used to build new ships, long-range bombers, and nuclear weapons. During Reagan's first few years in office, the United States spent more on weapons than it ever had before when the country was not at war. Reagan said that the Soviet Union was "going to be faced with…an arms race and they can't keep up."

Along with starting a new arms race, Reagan and his advisers sometimes talked about the ability to fight and win a nuclear war. The president seemed ready to shoot first and ask questions later—and risk the lives of millions of people. Protesters urged an end to the arms race and reductions in the number of existing nuclear weapons. Reagan, however, did not want to deal with the Soviet Union until he was sure that the United States had more nuclear weapons.

Troubles in Central America

Reagan and his advisers were positive that the Soviet Union and Cuba were trying to spread Communism close to the United States. Soon after taking office, he focused on two countries—El Salvador and Nicaragua. A small group of wealthy landowners had long controlled El Salvador. In 1979, reformers in the military backed a new government that wanted to help the poor. Wealthy conservatives and their friends in the army responded by supporting "death squads" that killed people who wanted reform. By 1980, the reform government was facing war with rebels who supported *socialism*, the economic system used under Communism. At the same time, the government could not control the death squads.

President Carter had given some aid to the Salvadoran government. He also sent military trainers. Reagan increased the military and economic aid. He thought that the influence of Cuba on the socialist rebels was the main cause of the civil war (1979–1992) unfolding in El Salvador. Critics said that the roots of the problem were poverty and the violence carried out by the government against its own people.

In nearby Nicaragua, a government friendly with Cuba was already in power. A 1979 revolution had ended the rule of Anastasio Somoza, a long-time friend of the United States. Carter had hoped that he could keep on good terms with the new government, led by a group called the Sandinistas. Reagan, however, was convinced that the Sandinistas wanted to install a full-fledged Communist government in Nicaragua. He cut off aid to the country and began arming Nicaraguan

Nicaraguan Sandinista soldiers pose with Cuban premier Fidel Castro in a show of support for the Nicaraguan government by the Communist leader.

Caribbean Concerns

In 1983, Reagan also saw Communism at work in Grenada, an island in the Caribbean. Grenada had a Communist government and received some aid from Cuba and the Soviet Union. Reagan feared that the country was building a new airstrip long enough for large Soviet cargo planes to use. He said that Grenada was "being readied…to export terror." Saying that U.S. medical students on the island were in danger, Reagan sent 6,000 troops there to install a government friendly to the United States. The attack marked the first time that U.S. ground troops had entered combat since the end of the Vietnam War (1964–1975). Most Americans supported the invasion. Soviet leaders saw that Reagan was serious about using force when necessary.

rebels based in neighboring Honduras and Costa Rica. These anti-Communist rebels were called the Contras. Trained by the Central Intelligence Agency (CIA), they carried out raids in Nicaragua, destroying property and killing civilians.

The people who forced Somoza from government were not all Communists. Many different groups opposed his rule, which kept most people poor and prevented any kind of democracy. However, once the revolution was over, the Sandinistas forced other groups out of the new government and eagerly accepted aid from Cuba and the Soviet Union. They also sent arms to the socialist rebels in El Salvador, though the Sandinistas denied this at the time.

Although Reagan saw the Sandinistas as a threat, some U.S. politicians did not want to support the Contras, who had ties to the old, hated Somoza government. Also, Democrats did not want the United States to take an active role in overthrowing the leader of another country. In 1982 and 1984, Congress passed laws, called the Boland Amendments, that forbade the CIA or the U.S. military from aiding the Contras. Reagan and his advisers chose to break the laws and secretly kept funding the Contras.

Violence in the Middle East

Like Jimmy Carter before him, Reagan hoped to bring peace to the Middle East. The situation there, however, had worsened since the Camp David Accords of 1978. The fighting was centered in Lebanon, where a civil war pitted Christians against Muslims. Adding to the violence were Palestinians, who used Lebanon as a base to attack Israel. Syria also played a military role in the country. Israel, meanwhile, attacked the Palestinians and supported Lebanese Christians.

Between 1975 and 1982, nearly 100,000 people died in Lebanon. In 1982, Reagan and his advisers finally managed to bring some peace to Lebanon. They convinced Israel to pull out of the country. The Palestine Liberation Organization (PLO), the main Palestinian force, also withdrew. About 800 U.S. troops joined soldiers from other nations to keep the peace.

That September, the Americans began leaving Lebanon but soon returned when new violence broke out. In October 1983, a terrorist bomb exploded outside a U.S. Marine base, killing 241 troops. Afterward, some Americans questioned the wisdom of having any U.S. troops in Lebanon. The U.S. forces were not large enough to truly keep the peace, and their presence upset Muslims who opposed U.S. support for Israel. The remaining troops soon went home.

During Reagan's presidency, trouble also broke out elsewhere in the Middle East. In 1981, during a training mission, U.S. jets shot down two Libyan planes after one of them fired at the U.S. aircraft. Reagan had already cut off relations with Libya, an Arab state in north Africa known to help terrorists. Five years later, Reagan blamed Libya for a terrorist attack in Germany that injured sixty Americans. The United States responded by bombing Libya.

A U.S. Marine stands in the ruins of the marine operations center in Beirut, Lebanon, in October 1983. The marine base was destroyed in a suicide bomb attack.

In the Persian Gulf, Americans watched closely as Iraq fought a war with neighboring Iran. The United States still had no diplomatic relations with Iran because of the 1979 hostage crisis. Iraq had attacked Iran in 1980, hoping to control some of its oil. As the war went on, the Reagan administration backed Iraq, sending economic aid. The United States also provided satellite pictures of Iran that helped Iraq plan its attacks.

The Iran-Iraq conflict lasted until 1988, and twice the war drew the United States into the fighting. In 1987, Iraqi missiles hit a U.S. naval ship patrolling the Persian Gulf, killing thirty-seven sailors. Iraq called the incident an accident and apologized. The next year, a U.S. ship thought it was under attack and accidentally shot down an Iranian commercial jet. All the people on board were killed.

Disaster in the Air

In September 1983, an incident over Korea added new tension to Soviet-American relations. A Soviet military jet shot down a South Korean commercial plane, killing all 269 people on board. The passengers included a member of the U.S. Congress. The Soviets claimed that the plane was on a spy mission for the United States. Reagan denied this and called the attack "a crime against humanity." The Soviet Union refused to admit that it had made a mistake. The shooting stirred anti-Soviet feelings in the United States.

Star Wars

By the end of 1983, Soviet leaders were concerned that Reagan might consider launching a nuclear attack on their country. A new U.S. program called the Strategic Defense Initiative (SDI) had increased these fears. In March 1983, Reagan called for research on a system that would use lasers based in space to shoot down Soviet nuclear missiles before they reached the United States. The new system was nicknamed "Star Wars."

If Star Wars worked it would end the old situation between the United States and the Soviet Union, called *mutual assured destruction* (MAD). MAD was based on the idea that neither country would launch a first strike against the other because it would be too risky. The country attacked would still have enough nuclear weapons left to strike back and wipe out the attacker. With Star Wars the United States could strike first and have a "shield" that could prevent a deadly Soviet counterattack.

Through the CIA Reagan learned about the Soviet

Noted physicist Dr. Edward Teller (left), one of the inventors of the atomic bomb, and General James A. Abrahamson (right), director of the Strategic Defense Initiative, clap for President Reagan at a conference marking the first five years of the Star Wars missile program in 1988.

fears of a nuclear attack. To calm these fears, he supported new efforts to reduce nuclear arms and improve Soviet-American relations. In September 1984, a high-ranking Soviet official met with George Shultz, the U.S. secretary of state. The talks went well at a time when the Soviet Union was facing changes in its government. One leader, Yuri Andropov, had died in February 1984. His replacement, Konstantin Chernenko, was in power for little more than a year before his death. Finally, in March 1985, Mikhail Gorbachev took control. He was soon ready to join Reagan in seeking new arms reductions.

Cold War Thaw

At first, Gorbachev tried to continue the old Soviet policies. He spent money on the military and sent more troops into Afghanistan, which the Soviets had invaded in 1979 in order to set up a government loyal to them. However, the war there was going badly for the Soviets, in part because of

Mikhail Gorbachev (1931–)

A dedicated Communist, Mikhail Gorbachev saw that his country had to change to survive. When he took control of the Soviet Union in 1985, he started a program he called *perestroika*, or restructuring, to improve social and economic conditions in the Soviet Union. He also proposed *glasnost*, or openness. He wanted Soviet citizens to have more contact with the rest of the world—something all past Soviet leaders had tried to prevent. Under Gorbachev, the Communist nations of Eastern Europe began to reform and move toward democracy. Many of the republics that formed the Soviet Union also demanded changes. Slowly, they began to declare their independence, and by the end of 1991, the Soviet Union no longer existed.

increased U.S. aid to the Muslim fighters resisting Soviet control. The Soviet Union was pouring its money into war and defense, while average Soviet citizens lacked food and consumer goods. Gorbachev finally decided that the Soviet Union had to slow down its arms race while still keeping a Communist government in power. He took steps to try to improve relations with the United States, including calling for a huge cut in each side's nuclear weapons.

In November 1985, Reagan and Gorbachev met in Geneva, Switzerland. Reagan refused Gorbachev's request to stop research on Star Wars. Reagan told Gorbachev, "You can't win the arms race"—a sign that Reagan was ready to keep spending on defense if the two countries could not reach agreements. At one point, Gorbachev told his aides that Reagan was a "caveman." In the end, however, the leaders agreed that they should never fight a nuclear war and that they would hold future arms talks.

The two leaders met again the next October, in Reykjavik, Iceland. This time, Gorbachev called for huge cuts on different kinds of nuclear weapons, and Reagan agreed. Then Gorbachev said that the two countries should eliminate all their intermediate-range missiles in Europe— a move that Reagan had urged several years before. The two men seemed to be gaining steam in their effort to reduce the risk of nuclear war. Gorbachev said that the two nations could get rid of all their long-range weapons in ten years. "Well, why didn't you say so in the first place!" Reagan responded. He had the same desire.

The positive mood quickly soured, however, when Gorbachev brought up Star Wars. He wanted the United States to end its research on SDI. Reagan could not accept this. The meeting ended without any firm agreement between the two countries. Still, the leaders left Iceland believing that the United States and the Soviet Union had made progress.

The next talks came in December 1987, in Washington, D.C. Reagan and Gorbachev agreed to get rid of all their intermediate-range nuclear forces. Gorbachev, seeking

President Ronald Reagan shakes hands with Soviet leader Mikhail Gorbachev at their first summit meeting near Geneva, Switzerland. This was the first of three meetings between the two men that would lead to significant reductions in nuclear arms for both countries.

other ways to cut spending on defense, then withdrew Soviet troops from Afghanistan. In December 1988, he announced that the Soviet Union was pulling thousands of tanks and large guns out of Eastern Europe. He would also reduce the size of the Soviet military by 500,000 troops. By this time, Reagan had traveled to the Soviet capital of Moscow. He told a Soviet reporter that he no longer saw the Soviet Union as an "evil empire," as he had once called it. Before leaving the Soviet Union, Reagan said that he had "hope for a new era in human history, an era of peace."

The Iran-Contra Affair

Reagan's dealings with Gorbachev were the highlight of his foreign policy. The lowest point came before the president strolled the streets of Moscow, during the Iran-Contra affair.

Despite the Boland Amendments, which prevented the U.S. government from aiding the Contras, Reagan was

FAST FACT

Since the presidency of Richard Nixon, the ongoing Soviet-American talks to reduce long-range nuclear weapons were called Strategic Arms Limitation Talks (SALT). Ronald Reagan renamed the discussions Strategic Arms Reduction Talks (START).

determined to fight Communism in Nicaragua. Starting in 1984, the CIA and the National Security Council (NSC) led the efforts to get funds and weapons for the Contras. Some of the money came from foreign countries. A small part of it came from a secret deal taking place with a U.S. enemy, Iran.

Since the end of the Iranian hostage crisis in 1981, several other Americans had been taken hostage in Lebanon. Their captors had ties to Iran. Reagan had promised that his government would never make any deals to win the release of American hostages. Yet through Israel and on its own, the U.S. government sold weapons worth $30 million to Iran, starting in late 1985. Reagan's advisers hoped that the deal would persuade Iran to use its influence to release the hostages. Some of the money from the arms deal was then used to aid the Contras.

Lieutenant Colonel Oliver North, an adviser to the National Security Council, holds up a top secret NSC document during his testimony before the joint House-Senate committee investigating the Iran-Contra affair.

The Iran-Contra affair, as it was called, became public in November 1986. At first, Reagan claimed that the arms sale to Iran was not linked to freeing the hostages, which was not true. He also said that he did not know about using the money from the sale to help the Contras. John Poindexter, the head of the NSC, said that he had not told Reagan about all the details of the plan. In December 1985, Poindexter had replaced Robert McFarlane—who had played a role in the sale of weapons to Iran—as head of the NSC. The two NSC chiefs and a top aide, Colonel Oliver North, had directed the Iran-Contra operation.

When news of the scandal hit the press, Reagan's popularity fell sharply in opinion polls. In 1987, the people involved in the scandal faced intense questioning from Congress during hearings that were broadcast on television. McFarlane, Poindexter, and several other government officials were later convicted of various crimes, including withholding information from Congress.

In the end, no one directly linked Reagan to the scandal, but a report on Iran-Contra said that the president had failed to "take care that the laws be faithfully executed." The affair seemed to confirm that Reagan was not always directly involved in planning and carrying out important policies.

FAST FACT

In 1992, President George Bush pardoned the government officials who had been convicted for their activities in the Iran-Contra affair.

The Reagan Scorecard

At the time of the Iran-Contra affair, Reagan was seventy-six years old. His mind seemed to wander at times, and he easily forgot things. At least one doctor suggested that he might be suffering from the first effects of Alzheimer's disease. Alzheimer's affects the brain, causing a number of problems, including memory loss, difficulty performing simple tasks, and changes in personality. In 1994, five years after he left the presidency, Reagan announced that he did have Alzheimer's.

By then, historians and politicians were still debating the results of Reagan's presidency. He received credit for his efforts to end the Cold War. He also changed the way that people talked about the role of government. Conservative ideas were now readily accepted, especially the push for large tax cuts and limiting the role of the government in business. However, the Reagan Revolution had also led to the largest *deficits* in history—the government spent much more money than it took in. These deficits forced the government to borrow money. Money that could have been spent on new programs had to go toward repaying the loans. Further, Iran-Contra seemed a terrible example of a government lying and breaking the law to get its own way. Despite this, no one could deny that Reagan, the Great Communicator, had restored the faith of many Americans in their country.

George Bush

FORTY-FIRST PRESIDENT

FACT FILE

NAME
George Herbert Walker Bush

DATE OF BIRTH
June 12, 1924

PLACE OF BIRTH
Milton, Massachusetts

POLITICAL PARTY
Republican

VICE PRESIDENT
Dan Quayle

SECRETARIES OF STATE
James Baker (1989–1992)
Lawrence Eagleburger (1992–1993)

YEARS AS PRESIDENT
1989–1993

★ ★ ★

A Life of Service

Coming from a wealthy background, George Bush made his own fortune in the oil industry and then turned to politics and government service. His various positions let him travel and meet world leaders. By the time he reached the presidency in 1989, Bush was knowledgeable about international events. Few other presidents entered the office with that kind of foreign policy experience.

Bush's greatest challenge as president came in 1990, as he gathered international support for the Persian Gulf War (1991) to drive Iraq out of Kuwait. The war ended in a quick victory for U.S. forces and their allies. Bush also saw the collapse of Communism in Eastern Europe and the Soviet Union, which marked the end of the Cold War. In both cases, however, some historians have wondered if Bush could have done more to shape the events that followed.

From Wealth to War

When George Herbert Walker Bush was born in 1924, he entered a world of privilege that most Americans did not know. George was still an infant when the Bushes left Milton, Massachusetts, and settled in Greenwich, Connecticut. His father, Prescott, soon became a successful banker. George's mother, Dorothy, raised her five children to show good manners and not think too highly of themselves.

To the Bush family, George was "Poppy," a nickname that stuck for life. He attended a private elementary school in Greenwich. Bush then went to Phillips Academy, a private high school in Massachusetts. In 1941, Bush's senior year, he met Barbara Pierce. A distant relative of Franklin Pierce, the fourteenth president of the United States, Barbara eventually became his wife. Also, on December 7, 1941, the Japanese attacked the U.S. naval base at Pearl Harbor, Hawaii. The surprise attack drew the United States into World War II (1939–1945).

Bush was eager to graduate from Phillips and enlist in the military. On his eighteenth birthday, he entered the U.S. Navy. Bush trained as a pilot, and in 1944, he flew missions over the Pacific Ocean.

Oil and Politics

In September 1945, Bush was discharged from the navy and soon settled in New Haven, Connecticut, to study economics at Yale University. After graduating in 1948, Bush went to Odessa, Texas, to work for Dresser Industries. The company, owned by a friend of his father's, made equipment for the oil and gas industries.

Living in Odessa and then California, Bush learned about the oil industry. He then settled in Midland, Texas, found a partner, and started his own oil company. A few years later, Bush and several other partners formed the Zapata Petroleum Corporation. By 1959, he was president of the Zapata Off-Shore Company based in Houston.

Bush was helped by his family's business connections. He also had some political connections, as his father had been elected as a U.S. senator from Connecticut in 1952. In 1962, Republican leaders in Texas asked Bush to run for Houston County party chairman. Bush later wrote, "This was the challenge I had been waiting for, an opening into politics at the ground level, where it all starts." Early in 1963, his opponent for the position pulled out of the race, and Bush began his first political job.

The next year, Bush decided to run for the U.S. Senate, but he lost the race. Bush ran again in 1966, this time for the U.S. House of Representatives. He easily won the election. Two years later, Bush once again ran for the Senate. This time, he lost to Lloyd Bentsen Jr., a conservative Democrat. Since he had given up his seat in the House to run, Bush no longer had a job in Washington, D.C. He considered going back to Texas, but in December 1970, President Richard Nixon offered him a new position—U.S. ambassador to the United Nations (UN).

✔ **FAST FACT**

Through Zapata, George Bush had dealings with several international businesses, including an oil company based in Kuwait.

Representative George Bush meets with reporters in November 1970 after losing the race for the U.S. Senate to Lloyd Bentsen Jr.

Mr. Ambassador

As UN ambassador, Bush presented the views of the United States on a variety of international issues. He did not play a large role in deciding U.S. foreign policy—Nixon relied on Henry Kissinger for that. Instead, Bush established friendly personal relations with diplomats from around the world.

One important issue that Bush addressed was the problem of which China should sit in the UN. The Chinese civil war had ended in 1949 with an anti-Communist Chinese government in Taiwan and a Communist government on the mainland of China. This government was called the People's Republic of China. Taiwan held China's seat in the UN after the civil war.

In October 1971, the UN officially voted to give China's seat to the People's Republic of China. Bush thought that the vote to expel Taiwan reflected anti-American feelings among

The U.S. ambassador to the UN, George Bush (far left), accompanies President Gerald Ford (center) and Secretary of State Henry Kissinger (fourth from left) on a trip to Beijing in 1975.

some UN members. "It was an ugliness in the chamber," he wrote in his diary. "I was hissed when I got up to speak." The vote was also affected by changes in U.S. policy toward Communist China. Before the UN vote, President Nixon had announced that he would visit the People's Republic of China. With the United States willing to have better ties with Communist China, other countries thought that it was emerging as the true Chinese government.

Party Loyalty and Diplomatic Service

About two years later, Nixon had a new job for Bush. The president wanted him to head the Republican National Committee, the major fund-raiser for the Republican Party. Bush took over the party leadership at a difficult time. During the 1972 presidential campaign, the public had first learned about the Watergate break-in. The next year, the press learned more about the break-in and the burglars' ties to the Republican Party. As head of the committee, Bush traveled across the country, defending Nixon and the party.

However, Bush finally learned the truth, as did the country. President Nixon and his advisers had known about the break-in and had deceived the public about what they knew. By the summer of 1974, Nixon was facing *impeachment*—the legal process for removing a president accused of committing crimes. On August 7, Bush wrote Nixon: "It is my considered judgment that you should resign now."

The next day, Nixon did resign and Vice President Gerald Ford took over as president. When Ford asked Bush to choose his next job in the administration, Bush asked to be the first U.S. diplomat in the Chinese capital of Beijing. Nixon's earlier visit to China had led to the establishment of U.S. diplomatic relations with the Communist government for the first time.

UN Power

The move to expel Taiwan from the UN gave the People's Republic of China the Chinese seat on the UN Security Council. This council decides the UN's most important issues regarding war and peace. China has one of five permanent seats on the Security Council, along with the United States, France, Great Britain, and Russia. Any of these five nations can overrule a Security Council decision by voting against it.

✔ **FAST FACT**

In his role in China, Bush was sometimes called an *envoy*. In diplomacy, an envoy is considered one step below an *ambassador*, the title of a diplomat who represents his or her nation in a foreign country. Bush was not called "ambassador" because, at that time, the United States did not recognize the government in Beijing as the true Chinese government.

In Beijing, Bush met with Chinese officials, though not as often as he would have liked. He found the people friendly, though he disliked the lack of freedom in a Communist land. Still, as he wrote in his diary, "I don't think the United States has anything to fear from China."

Top Spy

Former Central Intelligence Agency director William Colby applauds as George Bush finishes remarks after being sworn in as director of the CIA on January 30, 1976. President Gerald Ford is at right.

Bush returned to the United States late in 1975 to take a new job—director of the Central Intelligence Agency (CIA). Of all his jobs until this time, Bush called the CIA position "the greatest of them all." Unfortunately, it did not last long. President Ford lost the 1976 presidential election to Jimmy Carter, and Carter wanted to choose his own advisers and officials. As 1977 began, Bush returned to Houston—but soon he would make plans for another political campaign.

Second in Command

By 1980, Bush was ready to run for the Republican Party's presidential nomination, but Ronald Reagan emerged as the party's choice for the presidential candidate. In July, Reagan asked Bush to run as his vice president. In November, Reagan and Bush won the election.

Bush showed his loyalty for eight years. During his vice presidency, Bush traveled to more than sixty countries. He represented the U.S. government and continued to build strong ties with foreign leaders. He also briefly served as the acting president for about eight hours in 1985, when Reagan had surgery and Bush had the president's duties. Reagan also gave him several specific jobs. He led a group that studied how to stop the flow of illegal drugs into the United States. He also studied ways to fight terrorism. Bush's report on terrorism said that the U.S. government would never pay money to win the release of hostages or prisoners.

That policy was ignored during the Iran-Contra affair. Reagan's aides sold arms to Iran to try to win the release of hostages held in Lebanon. Money from the arms sales was then used to fund the Contras, anti-Communist rebels in Nicaragua. Bush said that he was "not in the loop"—not one of the people who had made key decisions on these matters. However, some people found it hard to believe that Bush did not know more about the affair, since he was close to several people who were actively involved in helping the Contras.

The Iran-Contra affair hurt the public image of both Reagan and Bush. However, the vice president still remained a clear favorite to be the Republican candidate for president in 1988. In August, Bush won the party's nomination. He stressed his government experience, especially in foreign affairs, and he promised not to raise taxes. Bush easily beat Democratic candidate Michael Dukakis to win the presidency.

Investigating the Spies

In 1975, Senator Frank Church of Idaho led a committee that investigated crimes committed by the CIA and other U.S. agencies that collect intelligence. The Church Committee revealed that the CIA had illegally opened the mail of U.S. citizens. The agency had also dosed some people with illegal drugs without telling them, in order to test the drugs' effects on humans. The Church Committee hearings led Congress to place tighter restrictions on CIA activities.

FAST FACT

George Bush was the first person since Martin Van Buren in 1836 to win a presidential election right after serving as vice president.

Early Troubles

Calling for freedom and democracy, students surround police officers near Tiananmen Square in Beijing, China, in May 1989. These demonstrations escalated into an international crisis when the Chinese government sent tanks to disperse the protesters the following month.

Under Reagan, the government debt had grown tremendously. Most years, the country had a *deficit*—it spent more money than it earned. To face this problem, Bush had to break the promise he had made not to raise taxes. The government also had to spend billions of dollars to help banks that had failed in the years before. The U.S. economy began to slide during Bush's administration. Unfairly or not, many Americans blamed the president for not taking steps to solve the problem.

Bush, always more comfortable with foreign rather than domestic affairs, faced his first international crisis in June 1989. Hundreds of thousands of Chinese flocked to Beijing's Tiananmen Square, demanding more freedom

and democracy in their country. On June 4, Chinese leaders sent in tanks to end the protests; hundreds of people were killed and thousands were arrested.

President Bush had to make a careful response. In public, he attacked the violence against the protesters. In private, he wrote to Chinese leader Deng Xiaoping, whom he had met years before. He wanted Deng to know how upset he was, but that he valued a friendship with China. "I did not want to see destroyed," Bush wrote, "this relationship that you and I have worked hard to build." Chinese-American relations survived the crisis. Still, some Americans wished that Bush had done more publicly to show U.S. displeasure with the situation.

FAST FACT

After Tiananmen Square, George Bush sent several advisers on a secret mission to Beijing, and former President Richard Nixon also visited Chinese leaders. These trips were designed to improve U.S.-Chinese relations during a difficult time.

Cold War Conclusions

President Bush had better success dealing with the Soviet Union. Under President Reagan, the Cold War had begun to end. Soviet leader Mikhail Gorbachev had slowly given his people more freedom and improved relations with other countries. He and Reagan made plans to reduce the number of nuclear weapons that each country owned. Bush encouraged Gorbachev to continue his reform policies and the pursuit of better relations with the United States.

Since the end of World War II, the Soviet Union had controlled most of the countries of Eastern Europe. It forced these nations to accept Communist governments and follow Soviet policies. In 1989, Gorbachev finally began giving the Eastern European nations more freedom to run their own affairs. The changes started first in Hungary and Poland. Bush, who visited those nations in July, noted that in Gdansk, Poland, "there were all kinds of signs of affection for the United States."

Bush then made plans for his first meeting with Gorbachev. Bush also called for more cuts in weapons. By the fall, the call for democracy had spread to East Germany.

Polish president Lech Walesa receives the Presidential Medal of Freedom from U.S. president George Bush at a ceremony in the White House on November 14, 1989.

Germany had been split after World War II—the western part of the country was an ally of the United States, while the eastern part had come under Soviet control. The capital city of Berlin was also split in two, with a large wall keeping East Germans from entering West Berlin.

On November 9, the East German government allowed its citizens to freely cross into West Berlin for the first time in almost thirty years. Soon, people began attacking the wall with hammers, trying to bring it down. In Washington, Bush tried to stay calm during this tremendous turning point in the Cold War. "I keenly understood what the Berliners we saw dancing in the streets felt," he later wrote. "But…we had to be careful not to upset the process just as it began." Some scholars and other world leaders say that Bush was right not to say or do much after the Berlin Wall came down. Any strong action from the United States might have led the Soviet Union to stop the reforms. Instead, they continued to spread through Eastern Europe and the Soviet Union itself.

The next month, Bush met with Gorbachev on the Mediterranean island of Malta. The president indicated that he would send more aid to the Soviet Union. He also wanted to continue with the Strategic Arms Reduction Talks (START) begun under President Reagan. Gorbachev later said that for the first time the United States and the Soviet Union did not see themselves as enemies.

Military Muscle in Panama

At the end of 1989, Bush ordered the first military action of his presidency. Violence was rising in Panama, a country with great importance to U.S. interests. The United States owned and operated the Panama Canal. Any trouble in Panama threatened the safe operations of the canal.

Bush disliked Panama's leader, General Manuel Noriega. The general had declared himself the "maximum leader" of Panama and ruled as a dictator. His special police force had killed many people—including a U.S. Marine. Noriega was also accused of helping Colombian drug dealers bring illegal drugs into the United States. Bush was determined to end Noriega's rule and have him face charges in a U.S. court.

On December 20, 12,000 U.S. troops arrived in Panama. They quickly took control of the country. Noriega fled and U.S. forces chased him. After several days, the general gave up and was taken to the United States. Only a few dozen Americans died in the fighting, and Bush won praise from most Americans for his swift action. Others criticized the president for the death of at least several hundred Panamanian civilians. In addition, the new Panamanian government was not as democratic as some Americans had hoped, and drug selling and other crimes remained a problem in the country.

Change in Poland

Gdansk, Poland, was the home of Solidarity, a group of workers who fought for democracy in their country. The organization was led by Lech Walesa, who had been arrested several times for opposing the Communist government in Poland. To many Americans, Walesa was a hero for challenging the Communists. U.S. leaders had supported Solidarity since its founding in 1979. In 1989, Solidarity won Poland's first free elections since the start of the Cold War. The next year, Walesa was elected president.

FAST FACT

In 1992, Manuel Noriega was convicted of selling drugs and sentenced to forty years in jail in Miami, Florida.

The Gulf War

The next year, Bush faced a much more threatening foreign crisis in the Middle East. On August 2, 1990, Iraqi troops rolled into neighboring Kuwait, breaking international law. Iraqi leader Saddam Hussein claimed that part of Kuwait belonged to his country and that some Kuwaitis had asked for Iraq's help in overthrowing the Kuwaiti government. In reality, Saddam wanted to control Kuwait's oil. He needed money after spending eight years fighting Iran. He had also borrowed money from Kuwait that he did not want to repay.

Both Kuwait and Iraq had huge supplies of oil. The United States relies on oil from the Middle East to power its cars, homes, and factories. The invasion threatened to raise oil prices or cut off the flow of oil to the United States. Iraqi troops were now on the border of Saudi Arabia—a U.S. ally and the owner of the world's largest supply of oil.

Like Manuel Noriega, Saddam had once had good relations with the United States. Now, Bush was ready to use force to drive Iraqi troops out of Kuwait.

Before turning to the military, Bush first wanted to try other tactics. He asked other Middle Eastern leaders to talk to Saddam, and he convinced the UN to place restrictions on

Secretary of Defense Dick Cheney (left) and Chairman of the Joint Chiefs of Staff General Colin Powell (right) talk to reporters at the Pentagon about the movement of U.S. troops into the Persian Gulf region in response to the Iraqi invasion of Kuwait.

trading with Iraq. During this time, the president talked with many world leaders to gain their support, while also making plans for a military attack. By November 1990, more than 400,000 U.S. troops were in the Middle East. Soldiers from more than two dozen countries joined the Americans in a coalition, ready to fight if Saddam would not leave Kuwait.

The UN had ordered Iraq to leave Kuwait by January 15, 1991. When that deadline passed, U.S. bomber planes attacked Iraq, launching the Persian Gulf War, also known as Operation Desert Storm. By then, Bush was calling Saddam "the butcher of Baghdad." (Baghdad is the Iraqi capital.) The president convinced Americans that Saddam had to be stopped before he controlled more oil or threatened other U.S. allies.

The bombing of Iraq lasted several weeks. Then ground forces, led by the United States, needed less than a week to drive the Iraqis out of Kuwait. "We're doing something decent," Bush wrote in his diary, "We're doing something good." The coalition forces of the United States and its allies had suffered few losses. When the war ended in March, almost 90 percent of Americans approved of Bush's presidency—the highest rating ever for any U.S. president in a poll.

After the War

The Gulf War met Bush's goals: to force Saddam out of Kuwait and destroy large parts of his military. However, the president was criticized for not sending troops into Iraq. Some military experts said that the U.S.-led forces could have easily reached Baghdad and forced Saddam out of power. Bush argued that such an action went beyond the UN resolution that allowed the coalition forces to attack Iraqi troops in Kuwait.

Bush was also questioned about not aiding Iraqis who rebelled against Saddam. In February, he called for the

Sickly Soldiers

After the Gulf War, many U.S. troops came home with a variety of ailments and physical problems. Many were convinced that they had been exposed to something in Kuwait that caused their illnesses, which came to be called Gulf War Syndrome. Some experts said that the soldiers might have been exposed to small amounts of chemicals or radiation. (*Radiation* is a form of energy that can be deadly in large doses.) Others said that vaccines given to fight diseases might have caused some health problems. The U.S. government claimed that the soldiers had not been near any substances that could have caused their illnesses. By 2002, the U.S. government had spent $300 million researching Gulf War Syndrome but still could not explain why so many former soldiers were sick.

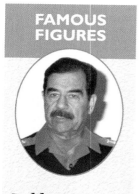

***Saddam Hussein
(1937–)***

Saddam Hussein was born in a small village near Takrit, Iraq. As a young man, he joined the Ba'ath Party, which promoted socialism and worked to modernize the country. In 1968, military officers from the party took over the government. Saddam played a key role in the new government, and he helped get Soviet aid for Iraq. He also killed anyone who seemed to threaten the government. Saddam took full power in 1979. He slowly ended the Ba'ath Party's influence, giving his relatives and people from his village more control over the government. In 1980, Iraqi troops invaded Iran, starting an eight-year war. Saddam's invasion of Kuwait started the Gulf War, leading to increased U.S. military activity in the Middle East, even after the war's end in 1991.

Iraqi people to overthrow Saddam. In the north of the country, an ethnic group called the Kurds soon began fighting Iraqi forces. In the south, Shi'ite Muslims took up arms against their government. (Saddam and his followers belonged to another branch of Islam, the Sunnis.) Saddam was able to end both the rebellions, as the United States refused to get involved. Later, Bush and British leaders set up "no-fly zones" over northern and southern Iraq. U.S. and British planes flew over these regions to keep Iraqi planes from launching attacks on the Kurds and Shi'ites.

At the end of the Gulf War, Saddam agreed to destroy his long-range missiles and destroy any chemical, biological, or nuclear weapons—*weapons of mass destruction.* He also agreed to let UN inspectors search for those deadly weapons.

Entering a New Era?

After the Gulf War victory, Bush talked about what he called a "new world order." The Cold War was ending, and many nations had come together to stop Saddam in the Middle East.

With the Soviet Union, Bush finally made a new agreement to reduce nuclear weapons. The two sides also agreed to reduce the forces that they stationed in Europe. At home, Gorbachev was facing growing problems. In August 1991, Soviet officials who opposed his reforms tried to take over the government. Boris Yeltsin, the president of the Russian Republic, led the efforts to preserve reform. By the end of the year, the Soviet Union no longer existed.

The collapse of the Soviet Union marked the end of the Cold War. For more than forty years, the U.S. government had confronted the Soviets around the world. Bush, speaking on Christmas Day 1991, noted that the United States had led the struggle against "Communism and the threat it posed to our most precious values." The battle against the Soviet Union was now over.

President Nelson Mandela (left) and Deputy President F.W. de Klerk talk outside parliament after the approval of South Africa's new constitution on May 8, 1996. Mandela joined the African National Congress in 1944 and directed a campaign against the government's racist policies. In 1990, de Klerk legalized the ANC and freed the imprisoned Mandela, who became the president and first black leader of South Africa. The two men shared the Nobel Peace Prize in 1993 for dismantling apartheid in South Africa.

The country had split up into separate republics. Most of these republics formed a new nation, the Commonwealth of Independent States (CIS). Later, the CIS broke apart as the former Soviet republics became independent nations. Most of them introduced democratic governments.

Positive changes also occurred in other parts of the world. For many years, South Africa had been ruled by a small group of whites who denied the legal rights of the country's large black population. President Reagan had limited trade with South Africa, hoping to convince the white leaders to end their racist policies. Bush continued these trade limitations. In 1990, South Africans elected a new leader, F.W. de Klerk, who began to make reforms. In 1991, Bush ended the trade restrictions because South Africa seemed to be moving toward greater democracy.

Nicaragua also saw changes. That Latin American country had been under Communist rule throughout the 1980s. Bush, like Reagan, supported anti-Communist rebels there. In 1990, a pro-American candidate, Violeta Barrios de Chamorro, won a presidential election, bringing the country's civil war (1980–1990) to an end.

FAST FACT

The South African system based on race was called *apartheid*. Society was clearly divided along racial lines, with the whites holding most power, followed by people called "colored." Most of these people were Asian or Indian. Blacks were on the bottom and were not allowed to vote, live in white communities, or hold certain jobs.

Problems Remain

In 1990, Yugoslavia, a Communist country in Eastern Europe, began breaking apart into smaller nations. Different groups within the individual countries struggled to gain power. Serbs, the dominant ethnic group in what remained of Yugoslavia, supported Serbs in neighboring countries, especially Bosnia.

In 1991, fighting broke out there between Serbs, Bosnian Muslims, and Croats, another ethnic group in the region. Some Americans feared that the war in that region could spread beyond its borders. The fighting also affected many innocent civilians, as they were driven from their homes. Some were tortured or killed. Bush, however, decided that the United States should not take an active role in the fighting, which dragged on for several years.

In Africa, a civil war was also going on in Somalia. The war led to great starvation, and in December 1992, U.S. troops arrived there to support a mission to provide food. However, Bush did not want the troops to play a long-term role in trying to keep peace in Somalia.

By the time the American forces reached Somalia, Bush was preparing to leave the White House. He had lost the 1992 presidential election to Bill Clinton. Some Americans were angry that Bush had broken his promise not to raise taxes. The economy had turned down in 1990 after many years of growth, and Bush was blamed for it.

Bush's greatest accomplishment, at home or abroad, was building the coalition that won the Gulf War. Even with that success, however, some people thought that, overall, he was not a strong leader. The world had changed dramatically with the end of the Cold War and new threats in the Middle East. Bush had not offered a bold vision for dealing with those changes.

Bill Clinton

FORTY-SECOND PRESIDENT

A Troubled Presidency

One of the most controversial presidents ever, Bill Clinton generated strong emotions. Supporters praised his intelligence and personal charm. Critics blasted his personal values, which created one of the worst political scandals in U.S. history. Clinton's lies about his personal life led to his impeachment in the U.S. House of Representatives. *Impeachment* is the legal process for removing a president accused of committing crimes. Clinton joined Andrew Johnson as just the second president to face a trial in the Senate for his alleged crimes. Like Johnson, Clinton was able to keep his job and serve out his term.

Clinton's foreign policy focused on many small outbreaks of violence around the world. He was willing to send U.S. troops overseas—if the risks were low—and he encouraged building coalitions to solve international problems. At the same time, he did not want these efforts to weaken America's national interests.

Early Dreams of the Presidency

Bill Clinton was born William Jefferson Blythe III, three months after his father was killed in a car accident. When Bill was five, his mother, Virginia, married Roger Clinton, and the family soon moved to Hot Springs, Arkansas.

A major turning point for Clinton came when he was sixteen. He was chosen to attend Boys Nation, an event sponsored each year by the American Legion, an organization of military veterans. For Boys Nation, Clinton went to Washington, D.C., and learned about the U.S. lawmaking process. He also met President John Kennedy. That meeting strengthened Clinton's desire to enter politics and someday run for president.

For college, Clinton went to Georgetown University in Washington, D.C. He majored in international relations and was active in school politics. He also worked part-time for Senator William Fulbright of Arkansas.

In 1968, just before graduating from Georgetown, Clinton received a Rhodes Scholarship. These highly

This 1966 Georgetown University yearbook photo shows class president Bill Clinton (left) along with Andy Poole (center, class secretary), and Terry Modglin (right, class vice president). Clinton's classmates at Georgetown have said that they knew even then that he would someday run for president of the United States.

prized scholarships are given each year to thirty-two U.S. students so that they can study at Oxford University in England. Clinton studied government at Oxford. He also attended several rallies protesting the U.S. role in the Vietnam War (1964–1975).

Clinton had worried about being drafted into the military just before leaving for Oxford. With some help from Senator Fulbright, he signed up for a military program at the University of Arkansas that kept him out of the draft.

FAST FACT

While studying at Oxford, Bill Clinton made a brief trip through Europe and the Soviet Union. Later, some of his political enemies falsely said that he had given up his U.S. citizenship during the trip.

Lawyer and Governor

Clinton returned to the United States in 1970 and entered law school at Yale University, in New Haven, Connecticut. There he met Hillary Rodham. They married in 1975. During his time at Yale, Clinton continued to learn about the political process and meet important people. In 1972, he managed the Texas presidential campaign of Democratic candidate George McGovern. Clinton also briefly worked for the House Judiciary Committee.

Earning his law degree in 1973, Clinton went home to Arkansas to teach law. He also started his political career, running for a seat in the U.S. House of Representatives. He lost that race, but two years later, he won the election to serve as Arkansas's attorney general. In 1978, Clinton was elected governor of the state.

During his first term as governor, Clinton raised a fee on automobiles and refused to go along with the views of several important state industries. He also faced a problem over Cuban refugees. The U.S. government was holding the Cubans as prisoners after they illegally entered the United States. About 20,000 of them were kept at a U.S. military base in Arkansas. In June 1980, some of prisoners began to riot and about 1,000 escaped the fort. Angry residents partially blamed Clinton for the situation, and other voters disliked his earlier fee increase. Clinton told an aide that the voters "hate my guts." Clinton lost his reelection race.

President Jimmy Carter shakes hands with Arkansas governor Bill Clinton at a campaign rally for Carter in Texarkana in 1980.

Clinton took a job at a Little Rock law firm, but he was already planning another run for governor. In his campaign for the 1982 election, he told voters that he had made mistakes as governor the first time, but he had learned to pay more attention to what they wanted. His message and his charm helped him win the election. The victory earned him a nickname—"the Comeback Kid."

For the next ten years, Clinton served as governor of Arkansas. One of his major goals was appointing more African Americans and women to government positions. He also worked to improve the state's schools.

☑ **FAST FACT**

Before joining the Council on Foreign Relations, Bill Clinton asked foreign policy expert Madeleine Albright to write him a letter of recommendation. Under Clinton, she became the first woman to serve as U.S. secretary of state.

★ ★ ★

Entering the National Scene

In 1986, Clinton was elected chairman of the National Governors Association (NGA), which studies how national public policies affect the states. Clinton also became active in the Democratic Leadership Council (DLC). Formed in the mid-1980s, the DLC brought together moderate Democrats. They wanted to move away from traditional Democratic attitudes that attacked large corporations and supported using the federal government to solve most problems. At the same time, the DLC believed that government still had a role in making sure that all Americans had the same opportunities to achieve success in their lives.

Clinton's moves were designed to make him a better candidate for president. He knew that he also needed to have more experience with foreign policy, so he joined the Council on Foreign Relations. This group welcomed members from any political party to research and discuss important topics in U.S. foreign affairs.

By the end of 1991, Clinton was ready to run for president. Not many Democrats were eager to run against President George Bush, whose popularity had skyrocketed right after the Persian Gulf War (1991). Although it began to slide a few months later, he still seemed to be a difficult opponent for any Democrat.

In his campaign, Clinton focused on domestic issues. The economy had slowed during the Bush presidency, and Clinton tried to suggest that Bush was out of touch with the problems that average Americans had. He also talked about the huge deficit and debt that the country faced. During the years that Bush and Ronald Reagan had sat in the White House, the U.S. government had spent billions of dollars more than it had received in taxes.

Clinton did not have strong competition from the Democrats for the party nomination. His biggest challenge came from his past. A national newspaper accused him of having been involved with another woman while married to Hillary Clinton. Clinton's avoidance of the draft during the Vietnam War also became an issue. Despite these problems, he won the Democratic nomination in July 1992. Clinton then went on to beat Bush in the presidential election.

Arkansas Scandals

Some of the questions about Bill Clinton's lifestyle and political dealings sprang from his years as governor of Arkansas. In 1978, he and his wife bought property with friends Susan and Jim McDougal, planning to sell lots for vacation homes. The land was soon called Whitewater. Later, Jim McDougal bought a small bank and used it to make illegal business deals. During this time, Hillary Clinton's law firm did business for McDougal's bank. The Clintons were accused of knowing about or taking part in McDougal's illegal dealings, including some related to Whitewater. Soon, the affair was known as the Whitewater scandal. While Clinton was president, the U.S. government spent millions of dollars investigating if he or Hillary Clinton had broken the law. They were never arrested, but both Susan and Jim McDougal spent time in jail because of Whitewater.

Troubles in Somalia

As president, Clinton advocated a tax increase and spending cuts to eliminate the federal deficit. He also wanted to help all Americans afford some form of health care. Clinton also pushed for a new crime law that outlawed certain kinds of assault weapons, high-powered guns normally used by the police or military.

Many of Clinton's spending cuts came in the military. With the Cold War over, Clinton and his advisers thought that some of the money that had been used for troops and weapons could now be used for domestic programs. However, the United States was still involved in several military actions around the world.

One troubled country was Somalia in East Africa, where fighting between small, private armies had led to a chaotic civil war. The most powerful military leader was Mohamed Aidid. The fighting, along with a drought, brought mass starvation to Somalia. In 1992, President Bush had sent troops to Somalia to protect aid workers distributing food. Gradually, the political situation in

Crowds throw stones at a passing U.S. Army forklift truck in Mogadishu, Somalia, to protest the presence of the U.S. military in their city in 1993.

Somalia began to improve. The so-called warlords who led the clans and tribes in the civil war began to discuss peace. In 1993, Clinton pulled out some U.S. troops as United Nations (UN) peacekeepers came to Somalia.

In June 1993, forces under Aidid attacked and killed UN troops. The United States then tried to hunt down and kill the warlord. That mission failed, and Aidid's forces continued to attack both UN and U.S. troops. The worst fighting came in October, when specially trained U.S. troops tried to capture Aidid. Nineteen Americans died in the unsuccessful raid, and jubilant Somalis celebrated over their dead bodies. When Clinton saw the scene on TV, he said, "It turned my stomach." After the disastrous raid, the president sent more troops to Somalia, but the move was not popular with most Americans. Early in 1994, the soldiers came home.

FAST FACT

The deadly October 1993 raid in Somalia was the subject of a 2001 film, *Black Hawk Down*. The movie was based on a book of the same name.

Troops in Haiti

Closer to the United States, Clinton was concerned with events in Haiti. A former French colony, Haiti had been the first Caribbean nation to declare its independence, in 1804. The country had never developed a strong economy or a democratic government, and violence sometimes broke out.

Starting in 1957, the Duvalier family ran Haiti. They controlled the economy and the government and used a brutal police force to imprison or kill any opponents.

The Duvaliers were finally forced out of power in 1986, and four years later, Haiti had its first democratic election. The winner was Jean-Bertrand Aristide, a former priest who wanted to reform the economy. In 1991, however, Haitian military officers led by Raul Cedras took over the government. The new government once again used violence to limit any opposition to its rule. Thousands of Haitians began fleeing the island in small, unsafe boats, heading for the United States. President Bush had said that

Troops of the army's 10th Mountain Division prepare to depart for Haiti following President Clinton's order to use the U.S. military to force Raul Cedras from office in that island nation.

the country could not accept the Haitian refugees and ordered them sent back to Haiti.

Clinton wanted to welcome the refugees, but the Central Intelligence Agency (CIA) told him that a massive new wave was about to leave Haiti for Florida. Many Americans did not want to take in up to 200,000 poor refugees. Clinton kept the Bush policy of sending back the refugees.

In July 1993, Cedras agreed to let Aristide return to Haiti as president. During the next few months, however, Cedras showed that he was not serious about his offer. Then in October, a ship carrying about 200 U.S. troops and two dozen Canadian engineers tried to land in Haiti. A mob organized by Cedras met the ship at the dock. Clinton and his advisers debated sending in more troops so that the ship could land safely, but the incident took place right after the failed raid in Somalia. After that loss, most of Clinton's advisers did not want another battle. Clinton decided to call back the ship. To many Americans, it looked like a poor, tiny nation had forced the United States to back down.

The next year, Clinton decided to use the military to force Cedras from power. As about 20,000 troops sailed for Haiti, Cedras realized that he faced defeat, and he agreed to turn over the government to Aristide. By then, Clinton had been accused of being weak in his foreign policy. A few years later, when he faced another risky situation, he said, "I'm never going to wimp out like I did in Haiti again."

Yugoslavia's Devastating War

Somalia and Haiti were difficult situations, but Clinton faced an even deadlier crisis in Yugoslavia. When that former Communist nation began to break apart in 1991, fighting broke out in several places. The worst conflict came in Bosnia-Herzegovina, where different ethnic groups battled for control. At times, Bosnia's Muslims and Croats united to fight the country's Serbs, who received support from Serbia, the largest republic left in Yugoslavia. At other times, the Croats and Muslims fought each other.

Clinton faced growing pressure to take action as the fighting went on. By 1993, as many as 150,000 people had died in the former Yugoslav republics. Some U.S. and European leaders wanted the United States to take military action against the Bosnian Serbs and Serbia, which now controlled most of Bosnia. Clinton refused, hoping the UN and the North Atlantic Treaty Organization (NATO) could end the fighting. The UN sent peacekeeping troops and set up "safe havens" where civilians could go to avoid the fighting. NATO used its planes to protect the peacekeepers and the safe havens. NATO planes—often flown by Americans—struck Bosnian Serb targets in 1994 and 1995. The Croats and Muslims began to gain ground against the Serbs. In the fall, Croatian, Bosnian Muslim, and Serb leaders met in Dayton, Ohio, to discuss peace. The agreement that they signed, the Dayton Accords, ended the fighting in Bosnia.

No Action in Rwanda

After the trouble in Somalia, Bill Clinton was reluctant to get involved in another African crisis. In April 1994, a civil war (1994–1996) broke out in Rwanda between members of rival tribes, the Hutus and Tutsis. Within three months, about 800,000 people were killed. Despite some calls for the United States to send troops, Clinton did not take action until most of the killing had stopped. In July, he sent several hundred soldiers to Rwanda to aid relief efforts. Later, Clinton seemed to indicate that the United States should have done something to stop the killing—but he never apologized for the lack of involvement during the massacre.

A British United Nations peacekeeper stands guard in front of armored vehicles near a Bosnian village in 1995. The UN force sent to establish order in the former country of Yugoslavia included U.S. troops and those of other nations.

A few years later, violence broke out in Serbia. Some ethnic Albanians in a region of the country called Kosovo were demanding their independence. They were led by the Kosovo Liberation Army, which sometimes attacked Serbian targets. In response, Serbian leader Slobodan Milosevic imprisoned and murdered the Albanians, also known as Kosovars. When Milosevic ignored NATO's calls to stop the violence, the Europeans and Americans began heavy bombing of Serb targets. Hundreds of thousands of refugees fled to Albania and Macedonia to escape the fighting. In 1999, NATO strikes led by the United States finally forced Milosevic to end the attacks on the Kosovars. As in Bosnia, U.S. troops joined an international force sent to keep the peace in Kosovo.

War and Peace in the Middle East

Iraqi leader Saddam Hussein also created new problems for the United States. In April 1993, Iraq organized a plot to assassinate former president Bush during a visit to Kuwait. When Clinton learned of the plan, he ordered a missile attack on the Iraqi capital, Baghdad. The next year, Saddam sent Iraqi troops close to the Kuwaiti border. The United States sent 36,000 troops to Kuwait and told Saddam to pull back his troops, which he did, rather than risk further violence.

During this time, UN weapons inspectors were searching for weapons of mass destruction in Iraq. Saddam made their job difficult by preventing them from entering certain areas. In 1998, Clinton twice ordered U.S. troops to the Persian Gulf to try to force Saddam to let the inspectors do their job. Saddam still refused to cooperate. That December, the inspectors left Iraq, and the United States and Great Britain attacked the country. Clinton said, "Saddam Hussein must not be allowed to threaten his neighbors or the world with nuclear arms, poison gas or biological weapons." The bomb and missile attacks hit Iraqi missile sites and other military targets.

The Israeli-Palestinian conflict also remained a major concern for the United States. In 1993, Clinton hosted Palestinian leader Yasir Arafat and Israeli prime minister Yitzhak Rabin in Washington, D.C. The two leaders signed an agreement that would let the Palestinians have some control over their own affairs in the Gaza Strip and the West Bank, areas under Israeli control. The Palestinians also agreed that Israel had a legal right to exist as an independent country—a right that they had rejected before. Rabin's efforts to improve relations with the Palestinians upset some Israelis. In 1995, Rabin was assassinated by an Israeli extremist.

In 1998, a new Israeli prime minister, Benjamin Netanyahu, met with Clinton and Arafat at the Wye

President Bill Clinton stands between Israeli prime minister Yitzhak Rabin (left) and Palestine Liberation Organization leader Yasser Arafat after the two leaders signed the 1993 peace accord.

Plantation in eastern Maryland. Clinton watched as the two men signed another important document. This Wye Agreement put more territory under Palestinian control. In return, Arafat was supposed to take stronger measures against terrorists who threatened Israel. Clinton tried to help the two sides complete a broader peace treaty in 2000, but the talks failed.

★ ★ ★

The New Russia

By the time that Clinton took office, the Soviet Union had broken apart. Still, Russia, the largest of the old Soviet republics, remained a concern for U.S. leaders. Its president, Boris Yeltsin, was trying to bring free enterprise and democracy to his country. Clinton wanted him to succeed in order to make sure that Communists did not return to power. Clinton was also concerned about the

FAST FACT

The Russian parliament finally approved START II in 2000, and first talks on START III began soon after.

nuclear weapons controlled by Russia and several other former Soviet republics.

Ukraine was a particular problem. With the collapse of the Soviet Union, Ukraine controlled more than 1,500 nuclear weapons. Under the first Strategic Arms Reduction Talks (START I), an arms agreement signed by George Bush and Mikhail Gorbachev, these missiles were supposed to be destroyed. However, the Ukrainian government feared a future Russian attack and thought that it would need the missiles for self-defense. The United States convinced Ukraine to give up the missiles in return for financial aid and guarantees to help protect its independence.

A second arms agreement, START II, had also been worked out under Bush. The U.S. Senate approved it in 1996, but Russian lawmakers were not pleased with the treaty's large cuts in nuclear weapons. With no action on START II, talks for START III stalled.

By September 1994, Clinton had realized that the United States had more nuclear weapons than it needed. "The Cold War is supposed to be over," he said. "What do we need this much overkill for?" Clinton thought about cutting the number of weapons *unilaterally*—without any Russian involvement. A U.S. law, however, limited his ability to reduce the number of weapons below the limits set out in START I.

Starting in 1994, Russia faced a rebellion in a region called Chechnya. When Clinton questioned Russian actions, Yeltsin and the next Russian president, Vladimir Putin, said that the rebellion was their problem, not America's—in other words, the United States should not question Russia's actions in Chechnya.

The war in Yugoslavia also tested the relationship between Clinton and the Russians. Russia protested U.S. bombings of Serbia in 1995 and 1999. When the fighting in Kosovo ended, the Russians broke an agreement with NATO. The two sides had said that they would send their peacekeeping forces into the region at the same time.

FAST FACT

After the Dayton Accords, 20,000 U.S. troops went to Bosnia as part of a NATO peacekeeping mission. The number of troops there was later reduced, but some remained in Bosnia as of 2003.

Missile Defense

Under President Ronald Reagan, the United States had started its Star Wars program—research on a space-based system that could prevent an enemy's nuclear missiles from reaching the United States. President Clinton focused on a land-based system called National Missile Defense. Both programs, if put into use, would break the 1972 Anti-Ballistic Missile (ABM) treaty between the United States and the Soviet Union (or Russia). In 2000, Clinton decided to stop work on the missile defense. He left it up to future presidents to decide if they would stick with the ABM treaty.

President Bill Clinton greets Russian KFOR troops on his arrival at Pristina, Kosovo, in November 1999, five months after NATO broke Serbia's grip on Kosovo. Clinton urged Kosovo's schoolchildren to forgive oppression and told U.S. peacekeeping soldiers that their example could help overcome the sectarian violence that still gripped the province.

Russia and NATO

Russia was suspicious about Eastern European nations joining NATO, but it did agree to have its own relationship with the organization. In 1991, it joined a new organization called the North Atlantic Cooperation Council. After this, Russia sent its troops on NATO peacekeeping missions and later agreed to work with NATO against common enemies.

Instead, the Russians went in on their own. The Russians wanted to assert themselves after not being able to help their Serbian allies. For a brief time, the incident threatened to lead to violence, but NATO troops entered Kosovo without any problems.

The end of the Cold War and the breakup of the Soviet Union left many Russians thinking that their country was weak. At the same time, Clinton was trying to improve relations with Eastern European nations that had been under Soviet control. Some Russians saw these moves as threatening their security. At times, Clinton talked with the Russians first, to make sure that they would not oppose his steps toward better relations with Eastern Europe.

In 1998, the United States approved expanding NATO to include Poland, Hungary, and the Czech Republic. They formally joined the military organization the next year. Clinton said the move created "a Europe that is united, democratic and secure for the first time since the rise of nation states on the European continent."

Terror at Home and Abroad

In the Middle East and parts of Asia, Islam is the dominant faith. Certain Muslims, sometimes called fundamentalists, strongly believe every word in their holy book, the *Qur'an*, known in the West as the *Koran*. Over time, some fundamentalists thought that Muslims had strayed from the original teachings in the Qur'an. They thought that the influence of the West, particularly the United States, was weakening Islam. To promote their vision of a "pure" Islam, a few fundamentalist groups turned to terrorism.

The first major terrorist attack on the United States came in February 1993. A group of Islamic fundamentalists left a van filled with explosives in the parking garage of New York's World Trade Center. The bombs damaged the Twin Towers of the World Trade Center, wounded a thousand people, and killed six. Clinton condemned the attack, but he urged Americans not to "overreact."

The next major terrorist attack occurred in April 1995, in Oklahoma City, where a bomb destroyed a federal building and killed 168 people. Americans soon learned that the attack was carried out by an American, Timothy McVeigh, and several of his friends. McVeigh opposed government actions that he thought limited personal freedoms. Even though there was no foreign connection, Clinton began to take a more serious look at terrorism. Still, the country could not stop the next series of terrorist attacks.

The first of these came in Saudi Arabia in 1996, when a bomb blew up outside a building where U.S. soldiers lived, killing nineteen Americans. Two years later, explosions killed almost 300 people at the U.S. embassies in Tanzania and Kenya, two African nations. By now, Clinton knew that a group called Al Qaeda was organizing terrorist attacks and training new terrorists. The group was suspected of carrying out the African embassy bombings. Later, it was learned that Al Qaeda had also played a role in stirring violence in Somalia when U.S. troops had been stationed there.

FAST FACT

One of the terrorists behind the 1993 World Trade Center bombing was Ramzi Yousef. Two years later, he planned to blow up almost a dozen U.S. commercial airplanes as they flew, but his liquid explosives started a fire that prevented him from carrying out the plot. He is now in prison.

The aftermath of the first major terrorist attack on the United States in 1993. The explosion in the parking garage of the World Trade Center left a crater 22 feet (6.6 meters) across and five stories deep.

Al Qaeda was led by Osama bin Laden, a wealthy Saudi who had gone to Afghanistan during the 1980s to fight the Soviet troops that had invaded that Islamic country. Bin Laden had now turned his hatred toward the United States, vowing to fight a *jihad,* or "holy war."

In response to the African embassy bombings, Clinton launched missile attacks on terrorist training camps in Afghanistan that were connected to Al Qaeda. Clinton told Americans, "With compelling evidence that the bin Laden network of terrorist groups was planning to mount further attacks against Americans and other freedom-loving people, I decided America must act." Clinton hoped to kill bin Laden in the attack, but the terrorist leader was unharmed.

The next Al Qaeda attack came in October 2000. In the Middle Eastern country of Yemen, a small boat carrying explosives pulled up next to a U.S. warship, the USS *Cole*. An explosion ripped though the *Cole,* badly damaging the ship and killing seventeen sailors. By this time, Clinton's second term as president was also over. The effort to track down the terrorists would go on under the next president.

Judging Clinton

Even before Clinton ran for reelection in 1996, many Americans questioned his personal conduct. After he defeated the Republican candidate, Bob Dole of Nebraska, new suggestions arose that Clinton had lied and acted in a way considered "unpresidential." The Whitewater scandal was still under investigation. He was also accused of having sexually abused a woman named Paula Jones while he served as Arkansas's governor. In 1998, evidence came out of a new sexual affair, with a presidential aide named Monica Lewinsky. This relationship led to his impeachment and almost cost him the presidency.

After the 1998 missile attacks on Al Qaeda targets, critics accused Clinton of using the attacks to take public attention away from his political problems. The same charge was made after the 1998 bombing of Iraq, when the House of Representatives was preparing to vote on Clinton's impeachment.

In the past, other presidents had been accused of using war or military action to boost their popularity, since Americans tend to support the president more if they feel that the country faces a foreign threat. Clinton's critics said some of his military actions served the same purpose, but the plan never really worked. Further, at times, as in Kosovo, he actually might have hesitated to take action because he knew that the scandals had weakened his relationship with Congress and the American people.

Clinton survived his scandals, but he left a mixed record. During his two terms, the economy grew and the

The Sudanese Connection

For several years during the 1990s, Osama bin Laden lived in Sudan. The Sudanese government follows the teachings of Islamic fundamentalists. Bin Laden set up camps in Sudan to train terrorists and started companies that raised funds for his activities. In 1998, President Clinton ordered a missile attack on a Sudanese plant thought to be producing materials for chemical weapons. In reality, the plant made medicines for both humans and animals.

Sudan has a mixed record on bin Laden and terrorism. In 1996, under pressure from Saudi Arabia and the United States, the government kicked out bin Laden. By some accounts, it had offered to turn him over to the Saudis and the Americans, but they had refused to take him. At the same time, Sudan remained on the U.S. list of countries that supported terrorism.

government was able to eliminate the huge deficits of the Reagan and Bush years. In foreign affairs, Clinton had some success using American military might to fight dictators. He helped build some international cooperation on key issues. He developed strong bonds with Russia and Eastern Europe. However, at times, he failed to act quickly on some issues, and some Americans later accused him of not having done all that he could to fight the rising power of terrorism. Overall, Clinton had the skills to do much as president, but his personal failures damaged him.

George W. Bush

FORTY-THIRD PRESIDENT

FACT FILE

NAME
George Walker Bush

DATE OF BIRTH
July 6, 1946

PLACE OF BIRTH
New Haven, Connecticut

POLITICAL PARTY
Republican

VICE PRESIDENT
Richard Cheney

SECRETARY OF STATE
Colin Powell

YEARS AS PRESIDENT
2001–

★ ★ ★

A New Bush for a New Age

When George W. Bush was elected to the White House, it was just the second time that a son of a U.S. president had also won the presidency. (The first occurred in 1824, with the election of John Quincy Adams, son of John Adams.) Bush relied on many of the same advisers that his father had used, though George W. was in some ways more conservative than his father.

When Bush was elected president, the United States was the world's only superpower, with the best military and the strongest economy. Bush thought that he could use that strength to take a *unilateral* approach to world events, meaning that the United States would seek to go its own way, rather than working with other nations. However, the events of one day—September 11, 2001— showed that even a great superpower faced serious threats. The terrorist attacks of that day made Bush realize that terrorism was an international problem.

Family Privilege and Service

George W. Bush was born in New Haven, Connecticut, the home of Yale University. His father, George H.W. Bush, had been a student there and had grown up in nearby Greenwich. After college, the elder George Bush took his family west, to Texas. Using family connections, he began a career in the oil industry and made millions of dollars.

Young George grew up in several Texas cities, including Midland and Houston. Starting in junior high, he went to a private school in Texas, and then in 1961, to Phillips Academy in Massachusetts, which his father had also attended.

George W. followed in his father's footsteps again in 1964, entering Yale. The year that George W. entered Yale, his father ran for the U.S. Senate. The elder Bush lost that race, but two years later, he won a seat in the U.S. House of Representatives. His political career would continue through and after George W.'s college years.

George Herbert Walker Bush (right) is shown pinning lieutenant's bars on his son George W. Bush (left), when the younger Bush became an officer in the Texas Air National Guard in 1968.

After graduating in 1968, George W. Bush returned to Texas and joined the Air National Guard, learning to fly jet planes. Bush spent a year learning how to be a pilot and then returned to Houston. He continued to fly and also worked on his father's 1970 campaign for the U.S. Senate. The elder Bush lost that race, but within a year, he had a new job: U.S. ambassador to the United Nations (UN).

The younger Bush spent many years, as he later said, "fumbling around." He applied to law school but did not get in. He worked briefly in the cattle business and helped an Alabama Republican running for the U.S. Senate. In 1973, Bush entered Harvard Business School in Massachusetts, but even after he earned his degree, he was not sure what he wanted to do.

FAST FACT

When George W. Bush was six years old, his grandfather, Prescott Bush, was elected a U.S. senator from Connecticut.

Business Failure and Success

Bush returned to Texas in 1976 and entered the oil business. The next year, he married Laura Welch. At the time, Bush was in his first political race, for a seat in the U.S. House of Representatives. Bush lost the 1978 election, but he saw the defeat as a learning experience. "Getting whipped," he later said, "was probably a pretty good thing for me." He then concentrated on the oil business. However, he did not duplicate his father's success in the business, and he pulled out in 1990.

In 1987 and 1988, Bush took time off from work to help his father run for president. The elder Bush had been elected vice president in 1980 under President Ronald Reagan. For the presidential campaign, George W. was his father's senior adviser.

The elder Bush won the presidential election of 1988, and his son later wrote that he "learned a lot about politics" during that race. George W. Bush then returned to Texas and pursued a new business interest, becoming a part owner of the Texas Rangers baseball team. Bush received extra

FAST FACT

George W. Bush helped the Texas Rangers acquire a new stadium in Arlington, Texas. He remained part owner of the team until 1998.

attention from the media because his father was president. With his political ties and his business interests, Bush was in a good position to seek a political office in Texas. His chance came in 1994, when he ran for governor.

Governor Bush

In the governor's race, Bush challenged Ann Richards, a popular Democrat seeking reelection. Bush faced one major obstacle: A Republican had not served as governor in Texas for more than 100 years. Richards held an early lead in polls of Texas voters, but on Election Day, Bush won, beating her by more than 300,000 votes. Many Democrats, as well as Republicans, supported him, and as governor, Bush crafted some policies that appealed to members of both parties. Republicans welcomed his tax cuts and efforts to reduce the number of people receiving welfare. Democrats liked the increased funding for public education.

Governor George W. Bush and his wife, Laura Bush, ride in the inaugural parade in Austin, Texas, following Bush's election to his second term as governor in January 1999.

Bush was easily elected governor again in 1998, and he continued to focus on education as one of his top concerns. At the same time, he and his advisers were already thinking about the presidential race of 2000. As that campaign began, Bush faced competition from several other Republicans for their party's nomination. They included Steve Forbes—also the son of a millionaire—and John McCain, a senator from Arizona. Bush had two major advantages. He was the son of a former president, and he could count on the support of many wealthy Republicans. He also came across as likable and trustworthy. He won the Republican nomination.

FAST FACT

In 1994, while George W. Bush was running for governor, his brother Jeb was seeking the same position in Florida. Jeb lost his race, but in 1998, he ran again and won.

A Historic Election

Bush's opponent in the November 2000 election was Vice President Al Gore. The vice president reminded voters that the Democrats had just led the country through a great economic boom. Gore tried to show that he had more experience than Bush and had a better understanding of important issues, such as foreign affairs. However, in an October debate with Gore, Bush spoke well on foreign policy issues, ending some of the fears that he lacked experience in that area. He also had a knowledgeable running mate, Dick Cheney. Under Bush's father, Cheney had served as secretary of defense. With that experience, he would be able to offer Bush useful advice on important foreign issues that affected the country's security.

On the other side, Gore had his own problems. Many voters associated him with the scandals that had arisen during Bill Clinton's presidency. Gore also had to overcome his personality—some voters found him dull and stiff when he made public speeches.

On Election Day, the race was extremely close. At one point, Gore seemed to be the winner, but the final decision depended on the election results from Florida. Both

Candidate George W. Bush visits a group of children at the Community Day Charter School in Lawrence, Massachusetts, during his presidential campaign in June 1999.

candidates needed that state's electoral votes to win the election. However, the results were questioned. In some towns, voting machines did not work properly. In other places, voters were confused by the way that the candidates' names were listed on the ballots.

Gore requested a recount of some votes. By state law, the Florida secretary of state had to declare a winner within seven days of the election, but the recounts were still going on. At this point, Bush was ahead by several hundred votes. After much legal wrangling in the state supreme court and the U.S. Supreme Court, on December 9, the U.S. Court ordered the recounts to end. Three days later, the Court overturned another state supreme court decision to allow some recounts. That same day, the Florida legislature voted to allow electors who supported Bush to represent the state at the electoral college. Under the U.S. Constitution, these electors, chosen in each state, choose the president. The vote in the Florida legislature meant that Bush would win the national election.

Across the country, more voters had chosen Gore than Bush, but under the electoral college system, a candidate becomes president by winning the electoral votes in individual states. Bush ended up with 271 electoral votes—just one more than he needed to win the election.

On December 13, Gore announced that he would not seek any more recounts. George W. Bush would become the forty-third president of the United States. That same day, a relieved Bush said, "The presidency is more than an honor, more than an office, it is a charge to keep, and I will give it my all."

Taking Stands—Alone

As president, Bush faced several problems. To some Americans, he was not the "real" president, elected by the voters. He seemed to have benefited from political ties and the rulings of the Supreme Court. He also still faced questions about his ability, especially in foreign affairs. However, with Dick Cheney as his vice president, Bush had someone close to him with knowledge in that area. The president also selected several other people with foreign policy experience to fill key positions. For secretary of state he named Colin Powell, a former general who had served as the head of the Joint Chiefs of Staff under the first President Bush and Bill Clinton. (The Joint Chiefs are the president's top military advisers.) For national security adviser, Bush chose Condoleezza Rice. An expert on the former Soviet Union, she had been an adviser to George H.W. Bush. Rounding out the team was Donald Rumsfeld as secretary of defense. He had held several government positions under Presidents Richard Nixon and Gerald Ford, including U.S. ambassador to the North Atlantic Treaty Organization (NATO) and secretary of defense.

President Bush's arrival in Japan in February 2002 sparked demonstrations by foreign residents who protested his rejection of the Kyoto Protocol climate pact.

Defense was one of the first issues that Bush hoped to address. He promised to spend more on weapons and increase soldiers' salaries. President Clinton had not made a decision on whether to pursue a system that could shoot down nuclear missiles heading for the United States. Bush strongly supported such a system—even though it would mean ending the 1972 Anti-Ballistic Missile (ABM) treaty between the United States and Russia. He said that the missile system would deter so-called rogue states from launching missiles carrying chemical, biological, or nuclear weapons at the United States. In December 2001, Bush formally announced that the United States was pulling out of the ABM treaty with Russia.

Another international issue that Bush addressed early on was the status of the Kyoto Protocol. In 1997, more than fifty nations meeting in Kyoto, Japan, had signed a treaty intended to reduce the production of so-called greenhouse gases, which harm the environment. Bush opposed the Kyoto Protocol, saying that it would force U.S. industries to

spend too much money cutting their production of the gases. In taking this stance, Bush opposed America's European allies, who supported the agreement.

Bush also pulled out of or rejected other international agreements. One would have strengthened a ban on chemical weapons. Another would have set up an International Criminal Court. Bush did not necessarily disagree with the aims of these agreements, but he thought that the treaties would harm U.S. interests.

The United States also seemed to be playing less of a role in the Middle East than it had in the past. New violence had broken out in the region, and it continued after Bush took office. He said that the United States was "very interested in working with all parties," but "first and foremost, the violence must stop." Bush did not take active steps to restart peace talks for several months.

Bush also showed signs that he was changing U.S. policy toward China. Some of his aides saw China as a major military threat in the years to come. Tensions between the two countries rose in April 2001 after a U.S. spy plane collided with a Chinese warplane off the coast of China. The Chinese jet crashed into the sea, while the U.S. plane made an emergency landing in China. The Chinese government refused to release the plane's crew until Bush apologized and promised to end spy flights over China. Bush refused, saying that the Americans had been over international waters, not China, when the collision occurred. In the end, Bush did apologize, but he did not accept responsibility for the collision. He also did not promise to end the spy missions.

✓ FAST FACT

The crews of U.S. spy planes—like the one that landed in China—are trained to destroy some of their high-tech equipment and the information that they have gathered if they are forced to make an emergency landing. In the China incident, the crew was not able to destroy all of the information before the Chinese took over the plane.

A Turning Point in U.S. History

Although he faced many international problems, Bush seemed more concerned with domestic issues as he began his term. The economy was still weak after a downturn during the last year of Clinton's presidency. Bush supported a large tax cut so that people would have more money to spend and invest. The country also faced several business scandals. Several large firms were accused of using illegal practices to make their companies look stronger than they were.

Despite these issues, Bush's focus quickly shifted to international events and national security on September 11, 2001. That morning, he received disturbing news. A plane had just crashed into one of the Twin Towers at New York City's World Trade Center. Within minutes, another plane hit the second tower. A third plane crashed into the Pentagon, in Washington, D.C., and a fourth plane crashed into a field in Shanksville, Pennsylvania. The fourth plane had also been on its way to Washington, D.C., presumably to strike at the U.S. Capitol or another government building.

By noon that day, about 3,000 people had died in the worst terrorist attacks in U.S. history. The country soon learned that each plane had been hijacked, or taken over, by small groups of Arab men. They had then flown the planes into the World Trade Center and the Pentagon. On the

Clouds of smoke billow from the Twin Towers of the World Trade Center after terrorists crashed two commercial airliners into the buildings on September 11, 2001.

fourth plane, passengers had forced the hijackers to crash the plane before it could reach its target in Washington.

U.S. officials immediately suspected that Osama bin Laden was responsible for the horror. His Al Qaeda terrorist group had carried out several deadly attacks on U.S. targets during the Clinton administration. Bin Laden had called for a *jihad,* or holy war, against the United States. He opposed the presence of U.S. troops in his former homeland, Saudi Arabia. He also opposed U.S. support for Israel. Like many other Muslim fundamentalists, he blamed the United States for threatening the traditional values of the Islamic religion.

The September 11 attacks focused mostly on civilian targets, not military ones. With these attacks, Bush faced a challenge that no other U.S. president had ever seen. The country was entering a war with an enemy that was hard to find. Al Qaeda had small groups of followers, called *cells,* around the world. The members blended into civilian populations wherever they lived. Still, Bush promised that "the search is underway for those who are behind these evil acts."

Almost immediately, Bush began planning for military action against bin Laden and Al Qaeda. The terrorist leader was known to be in Afghanistan, where he had set up training camps. The country was ruled by the Taliban, a group that shared bin Laden's views on Islam and the negative impact of U.S. policies and lifestyles on their religious practices.

The war on terrorism forced Bush to seek international help. Terrorists secretly operate in many countries, and they send funds over international borders. The United States needed intelligence from any government that tracked terrorists. These governments would also be asked to stop terrorists planning attacks against the United States or other countries. Bush, following the example of his father during the Persian Gulf War (1991), built an international coalition to destroy the Taliban and find bin Laden.

The Taliban did not pose a strong military risk. After more than twenty years of war, Afghanistan was poor, with

FAMOUS FIGURES

Osama bin Laden (1957–)

Born in Syria, Osama bin Laden settled with his family in Saudi Arabia. His father made a fortune in the construction business, and bin Laden eventually inherited several hundred million dollars. Bin Laden was schooled in a strict form of Islam developed in Saudi Arabia, called Wahhabism. In the early 1980s, his faith led him to Afghanistan, where he helped fund and train Islamic soldiers fighting the Soviet troops that had invaded that country. In 1988, bin Laden formed Al Qaeda, or "the Base," to help set up strict Islamic government around the world. Bin Laden and Al Qaeda began carrying out terrorist attacks against U.S. targets in 1992, working up to the hijackings on September 11, 2001.

few modern weapons. The Taliban also faced opposition from groups within the country. Still, the fighting there could be difficult, because Afghanistan is mountainous and the winters are harsh. The war also presented a political problem. Bush did not want the world to think that the war on terrorism was a war against all Muslims. The United States counted on the support of Muslim countries in its war. Bush did not want to anger Muslims who might have mixed feelings about working with the United States.

Actions at Home and Abroad

In October 2001, U.S. and British forces began attacking Taliban positions in Afghanistan. The coalition attack was called Operation Enduring Freedom. U.S. troops blended old and new methods in the war. Some troops rode on horseback to scout out sites to be bombed, while lasers and computers guided the bombs to their targets. By the end of December, the Northern Alliance, the main anti-Taliban group, was in power. Many of the Al Qaeda camps had been destroyed, and U.S. forces had discovered new information about the group's plans. Bin Laden, however, managed to escape, most likely fleeing to Pakistan. U.S. troops remained in Afghanistan to search for remaining Taliban and Al Qaeda troops. They also provided security for the new government.

The war on terrorism was not just fought overseas. Bush and his advisers looked for ways to defend against future attacks on U.S. soil. The president created a new position, the director of homeland security, to oversee the efforts of many different government agencies, including those that collect information on terrorists and that protect transportation and energy systems. New government policies increased security at airports, nuclear power plants, and government buildings. The U.S. Justice Department rounded up thousands of immigrants who might have been in the country illegally or had some ties to terrorists.

Some of the government's actions came under a new law, the USA Patriot Act. The law and other government actions designed to fight terrorism were sometimes criticized for denying the rights of immigrants who had entered the country legally. Even a few U.S. citizens were denied their full legal rights. However, Bush promised that the Patriot Act "upholds and respects the civil liberties guaranteed by our Constitution." He said that the new laws were "essential not only to pursuing and punishing terrorists, but also preventing more atrocities in the hands of the evil ones."

Bush and others worried that future terrorist attacks could be even deadlier than September 11. In the past, bin Laden had tried to obtain biological, chemical, and nuclear weapons—weapons of mass destruction. That fear increased when several Americans died after breathing anthrax spores sent through the mail. Anthrax is a disease caused by bacteria that often infect and kill cattle. (Bacteria are microscopic organisms.) If humans breathe in anthrax spores, they become sick and can die if not treated in time.

U.S. Special Forces soldiers ride past local Afghans in the town of Kunduz in August 2002. U.S. forces used modern military equipment along with old-fashioned methods in an effort to root out Al Qaeda and Taliban fugitives.

Several governments, including the United States, had developed forms of anthrax that could be used as weapons.

When the anthrax deaths occurred, many Americans suspected that terrorists were responsible. Although the government could not link the anthrax to terrorists, fears grew about more attacks with biological weapons. Bush also worried that nations that opposed the United States might be willing to give weapons of mass destruction to terrorists. In January 2002, he named three specific nations that were part of an "axis of evil": North Korea, Iraq, and Iran. Of the three, Bush felt that Iraq posed the largest threat to U.S. security.

Gunning for Saddam

Saddam Hussein had remained a sore subject for U.S. leaders since the 1991 Persian Gulf War. A coalition organized by George H.W. Bush had easily forced Iraqi troops out of Kuwait. The elder Bush, however, did not want to attack Iraq itself and try to force Saddam from power. After that war, Saddam launched attacks on Iraqis in the north and south of his country, tried to assassinate Bush, and fired on U.S. planes patrolling the region. Saddam also broke an agreement with the UN to let inspectors destroy his weapons of mass destruction.

George W. Bush entered the White House viewing Saddam as a major threat to world peace and U.S. security. He believed that Saddam was continuing to develop weapons of mass destruction and would give them to terrorists. The president could not show a link between Iraq and the September 11 attack, but he increased his calls to force Iraq to end its development of weapons of mass destruction. Eventually, he also advocated removing Saddam from power.

This effort to confront Iraq increased through 2002. Bush said that the UN should enforce the agreements that Saddam had made in 1991 to allow weapons inspections.

He and his advisers said that they had evidence that Saddam was working on weapons of mass destruction. In Great Britain, Prime Minister Tony Blair echoed these concerns.

In September 2002, Bush said, "Iraq has answered a decade of UN demands with a decade of defiance. All the world now faces a test…are [UN] resolutions to be honored and enforced or cast aside without consequence?" Bush said that he preferred to work through the UN, but suggested that the United States would act on its own or with its allies to attack Iraq if the UN did not respond.

Bush's stance sparked rallies for peace in the United States. Some Americans said that Bush's call for war was more about controlling Iraqi oil than destroying a threat to U.S. security. Others questioned the evidence that Bush used to show that Saddam was close to developing nuclear weapons. Experts pointed out that defeating Iraqi forces would be harder than fighting the Taliban in Afghanistan. Some said that the U.S. forces should concentrate on bringing complete peace to that country before turning to Iraq. Even some of George H.W. Bush's former advisers thought that the younger Bush should not talk too openly of war and that he should try to use diplomacy instead.

FAST FACT

In 1979, about sixty-five people in the Soviet Union died from inhaling anthrax spores. At a nearby plant, the Soviet government had been trying to develop anthrax to use as a weapon. An accident at the plant released the spores into the air.

An Iraqi official shows United Nations inspectors a propellant stabilizer used for military weapons. The presence of such chemicals is part of the evidence that President Bush says demonstrates that Saddam Hussein is building weapons of mass destruction in Iraq.

Despite these concerns, Congress gave Bush the power to attack Iraq if he believed that U.S. security was at risk. By the end of 2002, U.S. troops in the region were ready to attack, with more troops preparing for battle.

Other Threats

A possible war with Iraq also raised concerns about U.S. relations with other Middle East countries. The United States already faced continued anger from some Arabs for its support of Israel. Fighting between Israeli troops and Palestinian forces had continued. So had terrorist attacks on Israeli civilians. Bush blamed Palestinian leader Yasir Arafat for much of the violence, and he urged the Palestinians to choose a new leader. With a new leader, the president said, the United States would work toward giving the Palestinians their own independent nation.

Along with the Middle East, Bush turned his attention to Asia in 2002. In October, North Korea admitted that it had been trying to develop nuclear weapons. This effort broke a 1994 agreement between North Korea and the United States. Bush, focusing on Iraq, hoped that diplomacy could be used to convince North Korea to stop its weapons program.

The international nature of terrorism was demonstrated throughout 2002. Terrorists linked to Al Qaeda killed several hundred people with a bomb on the island of Bali. Smaller explosions took place in Pakistan and Tunisia, and U.S. soldiers in Kuwait came under fire. As Bush continued his presidency, fighting terrorism at home and abroad remained one of America's major concerns.

Glossary

accords—agreements between nations or opposing groups

administration—the officials and actions connected to a particular U.S. president

alliance—an agreement among groups of people or nations, usually for purposes of protection

allies—friends and supporters of a person or country

ambassador—a government's representative in a foreign country

assassination—the murder of a leader or other important figure for political reasons

atom—an extremely small particle of matter found in all substances

cabinet—a group of advisers to a president

campaign—an organized effort to win a political election

civil rights—legal protections for citizens

coalition—a temporary combination of groups who agree to cooperate for a specific purpose

Communism—a political system featuring one party that holds complete power and promotes socialism

conservative—a person who believes that the government should not play a strong role in the economy and should encourage strong moral values

containment—the U.S. policy after World War II intended to stop the spread of Communism and the influence of the Soviet Union

conventional weapons—arms that do not use nuclear energy for their destructive force

deficit—the result of spending more money than a government takes in

détente—the easing of tensions

dissidents—people who openly oppose their own government, especially in Communist countries

domestic—relating to events within a country

embargo—a government restriction on trading certain goods

envoy—a diplomat one step below an ambassador who represents a government in a foreign country

free enterprise—an economic system that encourages citizens to own property and businesses with limited government restriction on economic activity

fundamentalist—a person who strongly supports the basic, early teachings of a religion

fusion—the joining together of atoms to create energy

hydrogen bomb—a highly destructive weapon that gets its explosive force from nuclear fusion

impeachment—the legal process used to remove an elected official accused of committing a crime

intercontinental ballistic missile (ICBM)—a missile that can travel more than 3,500 miles (5,600 kilometers)—from one continent to another—carrying one or more nuclear warheads

intermediate-range ballistic missile—a missile with a shorter range than an ICBM, usually from about 1,500 to 3,500 miles (2,400 to 5,600 kilometers)

isolationism—a policy by which a nation attempts to steer clear of involvement in the affairs of foreign nations

liberal—a person who believes that the government should play an active role in managing the economy and helping the poor

mutual assured destruction (MAD)—a situation that exists when opposing nations have enough nuclear weapons to withstand a surprise attack and still defeat one another

nationalism—a strong devotion to or belief in the culture and government of one's own nation

neutrality—the policy of not taking sides in disputes among foreign nations

nomination—the selection of a candidate by a political party

nuclear—relating to the core, or nucleus, of an atom; relating to weapons that use the energy produced by the splitting or fusing of atoms

nuclear bomb—a weapon that uses the energy inside atoms to create large explosions

radiation—a form of energy released during a nuclear explosion; large doses can be deadly

radioactive—relating to the release of radiation

refugees—people forced to flee their homeland because of war or a natural disaster

resolution—a statement supporting a particular position

satellite—a natural or artificial object that orbits a planet

socialism—an economic system that features government ownership of businesses and a high degree of central control over economic decisions

superpower—one of a small number of countries with a large military force and influence over other countries

tariff—a tax on foreign goods being brought into a country

unilateralism—acting alone, without consulting allies

warhead—the part of a missile that carries a nuclear weapon

weapons of mass destruction—weapons used to kill large numbers of people; especially biological, chemical, or nuclear weapons

welfare—government aid for the poor, elderly, or sick

Bibliography

Books

Burgan, Michael. *Cold War.* 5 vols. Austin, TX: Raintree Steck-Vaughn, 2001.

Colbert, Nancy A. *Great Society: The Story of Lyndon Baines Johnson.* Greensboro, NC: Morgan Reynolds, 2002.

Dowswell, Paul. *The Vietnam War.* Milwaukee, WI: World Almanac Library, 2002.

Goldman, Martin S. *Richard M. Nixon: The Complex President.* New York: Facts on File, 1998.

Heinrichs, Ann. *William Jefferson Clinton.* Minneapolis, MN: Compass Point Books, 2002.

Johnson, Dary. *The Reagan Years.* San Diego, CA: Lucent Books, 2000.

Joseph, Paul. *Gerald Ford.* Minneapolis, MN: Abdo, 2000.

McNeese, Tim. *George W. Bush: First President of the New Century.* Greensboro, NC: Morgan Reynolds, 2002.

Nardo, Don. *The War Against Iraq.* San Diego, CA: Lucent Books, 2001.

Schraff, Anne E. *Jimmy Carter.* Springfield, NJ: Enslow, 1998.

Spies, Karen Bornemann. *Isolation vs. Interventions: Is America the World's Police Force?* New York: Twenty-First Century Books, 1995.

Sufrin, Mark. *The Story of George Bush: The Forty-First President of the United States.* Milwaukee, WI: Gareth Stevens, 1997.

Web Sites

The American Experience—Vietnam Online
www.pbs.org/wgbh/amex/vietnam/index.html

Clinton Presidential Center
www.clintonpresidentialcenter.com/

CNN—Cold War
cnn.com/specials/cold.war

George Bush Presidential Library and Museum
bushlibrary.tamu.edu/

Gerald R. Ford Library and Museum
www.ford.utexas.edu/

Internet Public Library—
Presidents of the United States
www.ipl.org/ref/POTUS/

Jimmy Carter Library and Museum
www.jimmycarterlibrary.org/

Lyndon B. Johnson Library and Museum
www.lbjlib.utexas.edu/

National Security Archive—
The September 11th Sourcebooks
www.gwu.edu/~nsarchiv/NSAEBB/sept11/

PBS—Frontline: The Gulf War
www.pbs.org/wgbh/pages/frontline/gulf/

Richard Nixon Library & Birthplace
www.nixonfoundation.org/index.shtml

Ronald Reagan Presidential Foundation & Library
www.reaganfoundation.org/

U.S. Department of State—
Foreign Relations of the United States
www.state.gov/r/pa/ho.frus

The White House
www.whitehouse.gov/

Index